50 P 2 $3.85

.50

THE

•

NAPOLEONIC

•

REVOLUTION

CRITICAL PERIODS OF HISTORY

Robert D. Cross, GENERAL EDITOR

ROBERT B. HOLTMAN

THE

NAPOLEONIC

REVOLUTION

J. B. Lippincott Company

Philadelphia   New York   Toronto

To Bill

PREFACE

Napoleon was not a man to inspire neutral feelings. Faced with a personality so dynamic and a career so far-reaching and explosive, men find their view of him colored by either intense admiration or equally strong animosity. Napoleon continues even today to stir the emotions; as a result, probably more has been written about him than about any other historical personage except Jesus of Nazareth.

The present volume is not concerned with passing judgment, with showing whether Napoleon was good or evil. To decide, for example, whether he or the British were responsible for the resumption of war in 1803, or whether he had always been a megalomaniac or became one in the course of his career, is not within its scope. (Certainly Napoleon was not always the same person with the same ideas, and it is a mistake to treat the man and his reign as though each were a monolith.) Rather, accepting the fact of his pre-eminence, I have attacked the problem of what difference it made that it was Napoleon who succeeded to the French Revolution. This book is not a biography, monograph, or study of his "age."

The first two chapters should be viewed as introductory. They present, first, the framework within which Napoleon acted, and secondly, an account of some of the high points of his career. Thus they acquaint the reader from the beginning with matters necessary to an understanding of the topics discussed in the later chapters.

THE NAPOLEONIC REVOLUTION

According to Goethe, "To make an epoch in the world two conditions are notoriously essential—a good head and a great inheritance. Napoleon inherited the French Revolution." The "Age of Napoleon" was an epoch; the world was significantly altered by Napoleon's passage through it. His goals led to numerous important changes, not all of them envisioned or desired by him. To deny that these innovations were the result of his period would be equivalent to denying credit to a scientist for a discovery he was not seeking and which was completely accidental. To debate what percentage of any particular change sprang from his fertile mind would, however, be useless; since he was the person in authority, he should receive either the blame or the credit.

The aim of this volume, then, is to examine the elements of the "Napoleonic revolution" and see how they came about; to show the effects of Napoleon's career, to reveal the extent to which things became different in France, in Europe, in the world, because of the influence of, or reaction to, this phenomenal man.

ROBERT B. HOLTMAN

Baton Rouge, Louisiana
June 1967

8

CONTENTS

MAPS and CHARTS

· I ·

THE HERITAGE OF
THE EIGHTEENTH CENTURY

When historians call Napoleon a "man of the century," as they often do, the century they have in mind is the eighteenth—not the nineteenth, which saw his great triumphs and defeats. It was the eighteenth century which molded him and whose heir he was. Of all its aspects, the rivalry of France and Britain, the Enlightenment, and the French Revolution did most to shape Napoleon's policies.

Napoleon claimed that he consolidated the Revolution in France and extended it to other areas. In order to assess this claim, it is necessary to put his actions in perspective, to know what types of change the Revolutionaries had already effected and for what reasons. We are not, however, interested in the causes of the Revolution per se—only in those aspects of the background which explain Napoleon's actions or had a continuing influence on him.

The Revolution was in large part a child of the Enlightenment of the eighteenth century. This Enlightenment had very special features: a belief in natural law, springing from the many scientific discoveries of the period since the Renaissance, but especially of the seventeenth century, and more particularly Newton's law of gravitation; a belief in reason so strong that the whole century is sometimes called "The Age of Reason"; a belief that the natural laws could be discovered through the use of reason; a belief that accompanying these natural laws were natural rights of man; a belief that through the use of reason and natural law man could obtain a paradise on earth in the not-too-distant future; and a belief in humanitarianism, that men were their brother's keepers.

Of paramount importance to the Revolutionaries was the reliance on reason. They considered it reasonable to advocate and enact religious toleration, but at the same time they had little use for supernatural religion; to them the worst kind was that which had a highly organized church and clergy. The Catholic Church was therefore a natural object of attack. When the sources of governmental income temporarily dried up, the Revolutionaries confiscated the church lands so as to have security for a new type of paper currency. Next they abolished the monasteries. And in 1790, with the Civil Constitution of the Clergy, the National Assembly (1789–91) made the clergy civil servants of the state.

The government expected all members of the clergy to take an oath of loyalty to the regime; this caused a split into juring, or constitutional, clergy and nonjuring, or refractory, clergy. At a later date, under the National Convention (1792–95), the connection between church and state was severed, and it remained so for some time after Bonaparte came into power. This meant that the clergy, which had been partly supported by taxes under the *ancien régime* and solely by taxes during the earlier phases of the Revolution, was now dependent on voluntary contributions. In the meantime the government had favored, consecutively, several types of religious activity, some of them patriotic and all of them presumably rational.

The reasonableness of the Revolutionaries further accounted

for their attempts at dechristianization, one aspect of which was a Revolutionary calendar adopted in 1793 but made retroactive to 1792. This was to be a "natural" calendar, but in this case Nature's voice was falsetto. The months were given descriptive names—but these were more applicable to the Paris area than to the world at large. In an attempt to obtain a more rational calendar than the Gregorian (and there have been reform attempts ever since), they had applied the metric system—first introduced during the time of the Convention—to the calendar and to the telling of time. The year, which was to begin on September 22, was divided into twelve months of thirty days each. Each month was divided into decades of ten days. The names of the three months of autumn all ended in -aire, of winter in -ôse, of spring in -al, and of summer in -or.[1] At the end of the year there were five (six in leap year) complementary days. In keeping with the classical outlook of the century, the years were designated by Roman numerals. This Revolutionary calendar remained official until the beginning of 1806.

A realignment of the administrative divisions was another attempt to apply reason. Certainly there had been little rhyme or reason under the old regime. Parts had been added to parts with no concern to eliminate what had become outmoded or useless. To an extent this situation resulted from the system of selling offices; the holders henceforth owned them and could not be dispossessed. The central government was chaotic. The theoretically absolute monarch was theoretically aided by six men we may call ministers and by four councils, each considered a part of the Royal Council. The largest effective unit of government in France was the intendancy, or généralité, of which there were thirty-four—one of them Corsica—in 1789. Initially the intendants in charge of them had been middle-class, selected

---

[1] The names of the twelve months of the Revolutionary calendar were, in order: Vendémiaire, Brumaire, Frimaire, Nivôse, Pluviôse, Ventôse, Germinal, Floréal, Prairial, Messidor, Thermidor, and Fructidor.

because they would be completely dependent on the monarch; by 1789 they were nobles. Aided by subdelegates in financial matters, they had unlimited authority within their jurisdictions. The generalities had been established to remove power from the provinces, which were carry-overs from the days when feudal lords might be as strong as the king. But the noble governors of the provinces retained their positions, and numerous localities had special privileges. One such privilege, in the outlying areas, was that of having a provincial legislature. The cities lacked self-government, but the rural villages had elected assemblies and paid syndics to lay down and carry out policies.

The Revolutionaries effected a complete revision of the administration. The generalities and the useless provinces disappeared, to be replaced by *départements,* which, as the largest subdivisions of the country, correspond roughly to states in the United States. In accordance with the dictates of the Enlightenment, Nature was to have her say: each department was to be based on and named after a geographical feature. It was also to be small enough for one man, a prefect, to administer efficiently and not to constitute a threat to the central government. Each department was divided into districts, each district into cantons which served primarily judicial and elective functions, and each canton into municipalities. Throughout most of the Revolution, these administrative subdivisions had a great deal of autonomy. Despite its decentralization, the new system gave France an administrative uniformity lacking under the *ancien régime.*

Another Revolutionary political bequest was the concept of a written constitution. France received its first one, which provided for a Legislative Assembly as the most important organ of government, in 1791, and this constitution remained in effect for one year. The National Convention had the task of drawing up another; its Constitution of the Year III (1795) established the Directory (1795–99).

Each of the first three Revolutionary governments had a unicameral legislature because the "philosophes," the publicists of the Enlightenment, believed in popular sovereignty and thought a one-house legislature was the best way to express it. Under the Directory neither the executive nor the legislative branch, now composed of a Council of Elders and a Council of Five Hundred, was supreme. Therefore, whenever they reached an impasse, a *coup d'état* seemed to be the only solution.

The ideas of natural law and reasonableness likewise found expression in the field of economics. The mercantilism which had prevailed earlier advocated strict regulation by the state in order to obtain self-sufficiency and to bolster the country's strength in time of war; the newer economic theories stated that the welfare of all was best served by the welfare of each, that each should be free to undertake any economic activities he desired because he was the best judge of his own economic interests. A Scot, Adam Smith, gave voice to these views in the British Isles; of more immediate importance for France was the school of the physiocrats, started by François Quesnay, physician to Louis XV, and including Pierre-Samuel du Pont de Nemours. The physiocrats, too, believed in what was called *laissez faire,* which advocated free trade and noninterference by governments as the best means of creating wealth, because then "natural laws" could operate unhindered. The physiocrats believed that land was the source of all wealth. They therefore advocated a policy of favoring agriculture rather than commerce and industry, and also proposed a single tax on land to replace all other taxes.

Although enlightened economic ideas were not adopted *in toto* during the French Revolution, some of them were made into law. In 1791 the National Assembly passed the Le Chapelier law prohibiting economic associations; the guild system was now a thing of the past in France. The old tax system collapsed of its own weight; under the National Assembly all people were made subject to taxation according to their wealth. (The clergy and nobility had been largely exempt during the *ancien régime* even though they owned, respectively, 7 and 20 per cent of the land in France.) The new and uniform taxes were to be imposed only by duly elected representatives of the people; France, like the American colonies, believed there should be no taxation without representation. Internal tolls and customs were abolished as unnatural trammels on commerce.

The bankruptcy of the government had been the immediate cause of the French Revolution, and the Revolutionaries, despite trying numerous experiments, failed to solve the government's fiscal problems. They issued paper money; although it enabled them to keep the Revolution going, a vast and rapid inflation caused hardship to many individuals as well as to the government, which eventually repudiated most of the paper. A forced loan fell through. Finances were among the many unsolved problems which led France to accept Bonaparte when a coup was effected in November of 1799.

The tax system was an attempt to put into effect the Revolutionaries' idea of equality, at least in the eyes of the law, that found its philosophical statement in the Declaration of the Rights of Man and of Citizen, adopted in August of 1789 by the National Assembly. In addition to equality in taxation, all citizens received the right to hold public office, and Protestants and Jews received full citizenship in the first two years of the Revolution. The judicial system was revamped so as to eliminate manorial and ecclesiastical courts and to provide for trial by jury and the type of open court procedure we know in our own country today. Not only did the judicial system become classless; legally privileged classes disappeared from society. No longer was the clergy a separate estate. The Revolution proudly abolished the feudal regime and the nobility who were its beneficiaries.[2]

[2] The feudal regime was a system of rights, originating in custom or contract, enjoyed by the nobles in their relations with the peasants and based either on obligations springing from personal relationships or on the system of landholding. During the Revolution encumbrances on land ownership were removed.

Despite the talk of and even steps toward equality, the *bourgeoisie* remained firmly in control during the revolutionary decade. Although the Revolution had been started by the aristocrats, who were themselves rising and saw in the fiscal plight of the monarchy a chance to regain powers for themselves, they lost out in the Estates-General to the delegates of the middle classes. The latter insisted, before consenting to the Declaration of Rights, that the constitution for which it was to serve as preamble should not guarantee equal voting rights to all. During the decade of revolution not everybody could vote at all times, and for most of those who could cast ballots, the electoral process was indirect. (The more indirect the voting, the more easily a minority could exert effective control.) In general, the basis of the franchise was property as revealed in the payment of direct taxes.

The ideals of equality and middle-class dominance occasionally conflicted, as in education. Everybody should have an opportunity to attend school, but the subject matter tended to further bourgeois interests. According to the plan for a national system prepared by the Convention, in order that all children might receive some education, the government would support as many as one fourth of the pupils if they were indigent. (Unfortunately, the vast majority of Frenchmen remained illiterate because the government did not have the facilities to put its plans into effect.) The schools were to indoctrinate as well as teach; the decree on the organization of public education stated that the primary schools were to teach reading, writing, arithmetic, and the elements of republican morality. The middle classes scored a victory in a later decree of 1795 by eliminating provisions that primary students should learn crafts, visit the almshouses, and help the old people and relatives of the soldiers.

Despite the illiteracy, there existed for the first time newspapers aimed at the masses. Their existence resulted from unprecedented majority participation in the government and a wider reading public. Propaganda, partly in the form of what later came to be known as "yellow journalism," could thus play a larger role than formerly.

Another feature of the Enlightenment reflected in the Revolution was cosmopolitanism. Enlightened individuals talked a good deal about the brotherhood of man, a brotherhood which tied in closely with their belief in humanitarianism. They tended to play down patriotism and to denigrate the rivalries springing from it.

The predominant cultural outlook of the Enlightenment, neoclassicism or pseudoclassicism, was a further aspect of the universalism of the period. It held that there was one universal standard of beauty—and even, it was thought, a uniform standard of government.

Although the men of the Enlightenment objected to excessive control of economic activity by the state, they paradoxically looked to enlightened despotism for help in bringing about the earthly utopia. Europe saw many enlightened despots in the eighteenth century—Frederick the Great of Prussia, the doctrinaire Joseph II of Austria, the insincere Catherine the Great of Russia, Charles III of Spain, not to mention rulers of minor states. Despots all, they sought to concentrate power in the hands of the central government. They had, however, a concept of their position different from that of the divine-right monarchs of the preceding period. They looked on themselves as servants of the state, and on the state as a paternalistic institution to promote the welfare of their subjects.

One reason for the French Revolution was that France did not have an enlightened despot ready to push through the necessary reforms. Louis XVI's unwillingness to accept reforms voted by the Revolutionaries led to the establishment of a republic in 1792 and to loss of his head under the guillotine early in 1793.

The fact that France was strong—politically, militarily, and economically the strongest country on the Continent—was sig-

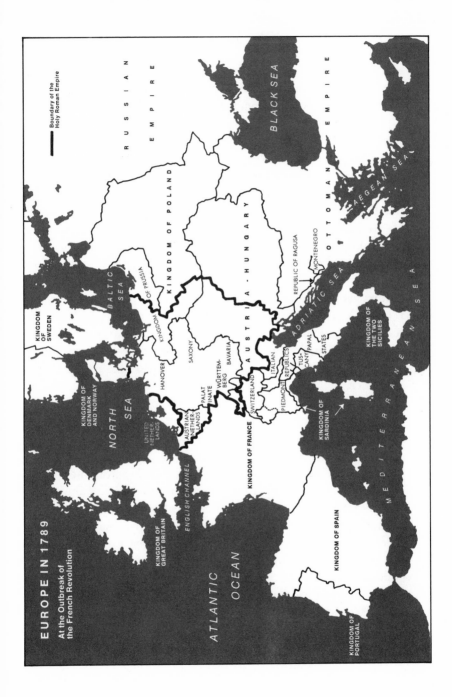

EUROPE IN 1789

At the Outbreak of
the French Revolution

Boundary of the
Holy Roman Empire

RUSSIAN EMPIRE

BLACK SEA

OTTOMAN EMPIRE

AEGEAN SEA

KINGDOM OF POLAND

AUSTRIA - HUNGARY

KINGDOM OF SWEDEN

BALTIC SEA

KINGDOM OF PRUSSIA

REPUBLIC OF RAGUSA

MONTENEGRO

ADRIATIC SEA

KINGDOM OF DENMARK AND NORWAY

NORTH SEA

HANOVER

SAXONY

WÜRTTEM-BERG

BAVARIA

PALAT-INATE

SWITZERLAND

ITALIAN REPUBLICS

PIEDMONT

TUS-CANY

PAPAL STATES

KINGDOM OF THE TWO SICILIES

UNITED NETHER-LANDS

AUSTRIAN NETHER-LANDS

ENGLISH CHANNEL

KINGDOM OF GREAT BRITAIN

KINGDOM OF FRANCE

KINGDOM OF SARDINIA

MEDITERRANEAN SEA

ATLANTIC OCEAN

KINGDOM OF SPAIN

KINGDOM OF PORTUGAL

nificant for Napoleon's career. France had a population second only to that of Russia. Though its government was bankrupt in 1789, its economic development surpassed that of the rest of the Continent. Unlike its neighbors, France was united. The countries of the Holy Roman Empire numbered in the hundreds and were of various types—free imperial cities owing allegiance only to the Emperor, ecclesiastical, and territorial—not to mention the myriad holdings of anachronistic imperial knights. "Germany" was therefore only a geographical expression. The same was true of "Italy," the states of the Italian peninsula.

But France was not so large as important elements in the ruling classes and the general populace would have liked it to be. They wanted for their country what they considered to be its "natural boundaries" of the Rhine, the Alps, and the Pyrenees. Louis XIV had tried and failed to obtain them; all that his two successors had acquired was Lorraine, when the father-in-law of Louix XV died. And Great Britain had consistently opposed a foothold in the Netherlands for a strong maritime nation such as France.

England and France had been enemies for so long, ever since William III of Holland became William III of England in 1688, that contemporaries considered their hostility to be permanent. In this rivalry Great Britain, able in a military sense to concentrate exclusively on maritime activities, had outdistanced its cross-Channel neighbor on the seas in the latter half of the 18th century. The naval strength of France had not kept pace with its strength on the Continent. The fighting between the two countries had been a major factor in bringing on the French Revolution, as it had contributed to the bankruptcy of the French government.

The warfare was renewed early in 1793 when Great Britain took the initiative in organizing the First Coalition. The immediate cause was the execution of Louis XVI; of more far-reaching significance was the proclamation in November 1792 by the French Republic of a "war of propaganda," not as we conceive it today, but to propagate the French system as widely as possible. After an initial series of defeats, France eventually won the War of the First Coalition. Great Britain refused to sign a peace treaty; but both Prussia and Austria, the latter unwarrantedly speaking on behalf of the Holy Roman Empire, agreed to the Rhine boundary for France.

The attempts of France to extend its control led to a second coalition in 1798, after the Directory converted Holland and Switzerland into satellite republics (the Batavian and Helvetic), established other such republics in Italy, and sent an expedition to conquer Egypt. Great Britain, Austria, the Ottoman Empire, and Russia had banded together to fight a new war—a war which France was losing.

This, then, was the background which made the time right for a Napoleon—the heritage of thought and events that would start him on his way to greatness.

· II ·

THE CAREER OF
NAPOLEON BONAPARTE

The defeats suffered by France in the War of the Second Coalition and the inability of the Directory to handle domestic problems satisfactorily do much to explain why the time was ripe in 1799 for an overthrow of the government. The Directory had been unable to restore the finances of the government to a firm footing. Economic activity lagged. The religious policy was unpopular. The Directory had continued measures of the Convention which tended to destroy family life. It had been unable to maintain order in the country. By *coups d'état* deemed necessary to keep the government running, permit the ruling elements to stay in power, and get out of impasses, it had violated its own constitution.

It was Napoleon, speaking in another context, who best explained the reasons for the establishment of his regime: "The truth is not half so important as what people think to be true." The people did not realize that the drastic measures of the Directory were in a fair way to improve the financial situation. To them it did not matter much that the French armies were faring better in the summer and fall of 1799. Most Frenchmen wanted a government which would preserve the Revolutionary heritage and provide a final victory in Europe. One group, the artisans, had become embittered about the Revolution and wanted it ended; Bonaparte's accession to power did bring to an end a decade of revolution. Some people welcomed the enlightened despotism; others did not recognize it under the cloak of legalism and constitutionality.

The change-over, welcomed by a big majority, was engineered by a handful of politicians who had become convinced that a root-and-branch reform of the government was necessary. Two of their number were Abbé Sieyès and Charles Maurice de Talleyrand-Périgord. They recognized that for a successful *coup d'état* they needed a military man. Bonaparte was not the first choice of the conspirators, but General Barthélemy Joubert had been so unfortunate as to be killed in Italy. Lucien Bonaparte made his brother their second choice after Napoleon returned from Egypt, unheralded and unannounced, in the early fall of 1799.

The coup was carried through on the 18th and 19th of Brumaire, Year VIII (November 9–10, 1799), with the support of the Council of Elders and the use of troops. Lucien, as president of the recalcitrant Council of Five Hundred, performed valiantly, in contrast to Napoleon's inept and wavering conduct.

Having seized control of the government, the conspirators had to frame a constitution. Sieyès, who had an unwarranted reputation as a drafter of constitutions, proposed to have three consuls (a title taken from republican Rome), one for foreign affairs, a second for domestic affairs, and a ceremonial figurehead who was to be Bonaparte. Bonaparte had other plans: he pushed through a constitution giving almost all power to a First Consul, chosen for ten years, who would of course be himself.

Who was this Napoleon Bonaparte who seized control of France? He was the son of a poor Corsican noble, born sometime in 1769, though nobody was quite sure when. Later he

27

declared August 15 as his birthday; the Feast of the Assumption seemed a good time for a Catholic nation to celebrate the birth of its leader.

France had annexed Corsica in 1768, and as his father was a noble, however minor, Napoleon was able to study at French military schools. At the age of nine—already domineering and obstreperous—he went to Brienne. Five years later he was able to attend the much more prestigious military school at Paris, and he became a second lieutenant in 1785 at the age of sixteen. He graduated forty-second in a class of fifty-nine, thus giving hope to pupils ever since, because he stayed only one year at Paris while most students attended for two or three years, and because he concentrated only on the subjects which interested him— particularly geography, history, and mathematics. All three greatly aided him in his career, though he tended to use history to justify his own purposes rather than objectively. Although his grades were low, at least one school inspector recognized an unusual intelligence.

When Napoleon had grown to manhood and become a states-man, there seemed to be almost no limit to his capacity for work; he could dictate simultaneously to several secretaries. He bragged that his mind was like a chest of drawers, that at will he could close or open the drawer of any particular topic. He read voraciously, usually with a purpose other than pleasure; the spirit of the eighteenth century strongly influenced his intel-lectual outlook. Though at school he was noted for his taciturn shyness, later on he developed a captivating charm. Always he was loyal, perhaps too loyal, to his family. Extremely headstrong and ambitious, he once remarked, "It is said that I am am-bitious, but this is an error; I am not, or at least my ambition is so intimately allied to my whole being that it cannot be separated from it."

In the early years of the Revolution Bonaparte did not con-sider himself a Frenchman, though he had received a commission as an artillery officer in the French army (and had risen to captain despite repeated absences without leave). He was still a Corsican named Napoleone Buonaparte, and until 1793 he devoted most of his energy to Corsican politics. By then his side had lost in what was virtually a civil war, and he and his entire family left Corsica permanently. He henceforth felt himself to be French rather than Corsican or Italian, and he subsequently changed his name to Napoleon Bonaparte.

Luck, as it must for all men, played a significant part in Napoleon's life. Not the least important time was in 1793, shortly after his return from Corsica, when France was involved in its Reign of Terror. Paris was decidedly more enthusiastic about the Terror than were the provinces, some parts of which were revolting against the regime of the Jacobins. One center of revolt was the great Mediterranean naval base of Toulon, where the royalists were aided by the British. The artillery commander of the besieging Republican army having been wounded, Bonaparte—en route to join the Army of Italy—was stopped and given charge of the artillery. He successfully positioned his guns to make possible the capture of the port. His plan was not unique, but he did have the ability and foresight to put it into effect. For the first time Napoleon Bonaparte had entered the spotlight of French Revolutionary history.

The light soon turned away, and he was temporarily left in the shadows. Suspected of having been too much the Terrorist, Bonaparte even spent ten days in jail when the moderates came back into power with the Thermidorian Reaction. Later he was dismissed from the army for refusing a command with the task of suppressing guerrilla warfare in the Vendée. He became a clerk in the war office. When the moderates drew up the Constitution of the Year III, the populace of Paris would not accept supplementary decrees guaranteeing that two thirds of the Convention would remain in office and staged an uprising on the 13th of Vendémiaire. Paul Barras, who was in charge of defending the Convention, summoned Bonaparte and five thousand troops to his aid. Later Bonaparte said that he dispersed the rebels with a "whiff of grapeshot."

Perhaps it was not quite that easy; Barras was sufficiently grateful to give Bonaparte command of the Army of Italy in the War of the First Coalition then going on against France. (Shortly before leaving on the campaign Bonaparte married Joséphine de Beauharnais, who had been Barras' mistress.) The Italian command was considered minor, but Bonaparte made it the most important of the campaign. The final victory of France over the coalition resulted in large measure from his brilliant strategy and tactics. Without authorization he brought the war and the coalition to an end by signing with Austria the Treaty of Campoformio in 1797.

Bonaparte was now the hero of the hour. He realized, however, that he would not remain such unless he kept in the spotlight with continued triumphs. The offer to head an army to invade England did not appeal to him. He proposed instead that he lead an expedition against Egypt, as a first step toward British India. The Directory agreed, in part because he had a powerful ally in Talleyrand, the foreign minister, and Bonaparte set sail in 1798.

While he was gone, the War of the Second Coalition broke out. This time Turkey and Russia were both members of the coalition—Turkey because Egypt was part of the Ottoman Empire and Russia because Tsar Paul had become Grand Master of the Knights of Malta, whose island Bonaparte had seized on his way to Egypt. Their adherence was an immediate result of the Egyptian campaign.

The most important long-range result of the expedition was achieved by the scientists and other learned men Bonaparte had taken with him. Some of these men founded the science of Egyptology, which was based in large part on the Rosetta stone, discovered on this expedition and later revealing the secrets of Egyptian writing.

Bonaparte had a monopoly on the news reaching France from Egypt; there was a minimum of communication because of the British fleets in the Mediterranean. He was able to create a false impression in France that he was consistently victorious in Egypt. While it is true that his inability to capture Acre was his only repulse on land, he had lost most of his fleet at Aboukir Bay.

Cut off from France, Bonaparte could not obtain reinforcements. He abdicated his command, recognizing his position to be ultimately hopeless, and set sail for France. There he shortly took part in the *coup d'état* of 18th Brumaire, completed by the Constitution of the Year VIII. This constitution established the Consulate (1799–1804).

The Consulate was the period of Napoleon's most constructive achievement. During it he laid down the institutions—administrative, financial, legal, and religious—which were to form the framework of 19th-century France. It is thus one of the most important periods of all French history.

Not content with being Consul merely for ten years, Bonaparte in 1802 maneuvered successfully to be named Consul for life, and two years later had himself proclaimed Emperor of the French. Pope Pius VII journeyed to Paris for the coronation, but Napoleon placed the crown on his head himself. Both as Consul and as Emperor he extended the control of France over European countries. The extension of control and annexation of territories were natural rewards of victorious wars.

His first consular campaign was in Italy, to end the War of the Second Coalition—and to consolidate his own hold on power. As a result of such victories as Marengo, won over a numerically superior force, Bonaparte was able to get Austria to sign in February of 1801 the Treaty of Lunéville. This reconfirmed the cession of German lands west of the Rhine agreed to at Campoformio. Russia had already withdrawn from the war because of disagreement with Austria. Great Britain, once again, was the only major country fighting France.

Even Great Britain came to terms with France in 1802, but

only for fourteen months. War between the two countries broke out again in May of 1803; in the meantime Bonaparte had annexed Piedmont and Elba. Resumption of the fighting with England, which continued until Napoleon was overthrown in 1814, led into a War of the Third Coalition in 1805. Despite British success in the decisive naval battle of Trafalgar, the war ended with a French victory at Austerlitz on the first anniversary of Napoleon's coronation (December 2 became the Bonapartes' lucky day) and the ensuing Treaty of Pressburg.

Napoleon could not remain at peace long. Even though Prussia started the next war, he brought it on by his eagerness to come to terms with Britain. He offered the British Hanover, and simultaneously took steps to weaken Prussia's position in northern Germany. In the War of the Fourth Coalition Napoleon easily, quickly, and decisively defeated Prussia in the fall of 1806 at Jena and Auerstedt.

Since Prussia's ally, Russia, showed a disposition to continue fighting, Napoleon had to move eastward. The first battle of the two land giants, fought in a snowstorm, was bloody, but left both unbowed. The battle of Friedland, in East Prussia, convinced Tsar Alexander I, in June 1807, that he should come to terms with the all-conquering "Little Corporal." At Tilsit they agreed not only on peace between themselves, but also on an alliance, which included a provision that Russia would join France in its economic warfare with England, the so-called "Continental System."

The year 1807 thus saw the height of Napoleon's influence, and it marked the start of his second great reform period in France. But the Continental System prevented his having the Continental peace he wanted. To be effective it had to be universal, so Napoleon began to plug the leaks. With this in mind he annexed such territory as the Papal States and northwestern Germany. The attempt to enforce the System required him to embark on a war in the Iberian Peninsula against Portugal and Spain which lasted five years and was a festering wound sapping his strength. While Napoleon was thus engaged, Austria in 1809 decided to go to war against him. For the first time Napoleon lost a battle, but he eventually defeated Austria and imposed the Treaty of Schönbrunn. He followed up the defeat of Austria by divorcing Joséphine and marrying Marie Louise, an archduchess and the daughter of the Austrian emperor.

The year 1810 marked the greatest extent of his territorial control, but his position had more brilliance than substance. At the end of the year Tsar Alexander announced that Russia would no longer exclude British goods. Both parties to the agreement at Tilsit felt betrayed (Alexander mainly because Napoleon had not aided him against Turkey) and therefore made preparations for war. In the campaign of 1812 Napoleon reached Moscow, which he thought the Russians would make any sacrifice to hold, but they refused to negotiate. Unable to spend the winter there, Napoleon ordered a retreat, during which his army suffered terribly. Only one sixth of the 600,000 soldiers who had entered Russia left it alive. Napoleon was now in decline. The "star of the west" was sinking in the east.

The campaign of 1812 merged into the War of Liberation in 1813, to drive Napoleon out of Germany and restore freedom of action to that area. The year 1814 saw the allies invade France, and move into Paris itself on the last day of March. Napoleon maintained that he had been betrayed. He negotiated an abdication treaty with the allies, who permitted him to retain the title of Emperor, but this time merely of the small island of Elba off the Tuscan coast of Italy. His wife refused to accompany him and took their son to Vienna.

Three factors, prodding his natural ambition, brought him back to France in 1815 for what turned out to be only a hundred days. One was the fact that he was not receiving the pension which the Bourbon king Louis XVIII was bound by treaty to pay him. A second was knowledge that Louis was becoming daily more unpopular in France. The last was a split among the anti-Napoleonic allies, who were trying at an international congress in Vienna to decide the fate of Europe.

As soon as they heard that he had landed, the allies patched up their differences and declared him an outlaw. This time, following his defeat at Waterloo, Napoleon did not receive the lenient treatment of the previous year. He had to spend the rest of his life in exile on St. Helena, a little island in the South Atlantic a thousand miles off the coast of Africa. There, until he died in May of 1821, he spent his time largely in feuding with his British governors and in dictating accounts of his ideals and activities. These writings went far to build up the Napoleonic legend which makes advisable a consideration of his impact on history—a sifting and winnowing to separate the false from the true.

· III ·

THE MILITARIST AND MAP-CHANGER

The name "Napoleon" almost automatically evokes a mental picture of a short man with right hand tucked inside his coat or jacket. Next arises the concept of Napoleon as a military leader —perhaps as a ruthless conqueror, perhaps as romantically pictured by court painter Jacques-Louis David, on horseback crossing the Alps in winter. (Actually Napoleon sat on a mule led by a soldier.)

That first thoughts turn to the military side of Napoleon's career is not surprising. More glamor generally attaches to the military man than to the civilian, and Napoleon was at war for all but fourteen months of the almost fifteen years he was in power.[1]

As early as 1817 the United States Army cadets at West Point began to study Napoleon in a course on "The History of the Art of War." Today Napoleon is still studied at West Point, where a

[1] The accompanying chart indicates Napoleon's major enemies and the periods during which he fought them. He was at peace with all countries only from March 1802 to May 1803. The war of Spain against Napoleon was guerrilla warfare, for Spain had no functioning anti-Napoleonic government; until early 1813 Joseph Bonaparte was on the Spanish throne.

knowledge of his work is considered as important in this age of nuclear weapons as it was earlier. In his biography of Napoleon, J. M. Thompson put very well the reason why military academies expound the French Emperor: "His campaigns have been made a textbook of military science; his strategy will perhaps always be magisterial."[2]

As the outstanding general in the last previous great war, Napoleon became the model for generals in the American Civil War. P. G. T. Beauregard became known as the "Napoleon in Gray," and others of the time would have liked to consider themselves new-generation Napoleons. Napoleon's military maxims were widely read in an English translation during the three decades preceding the war; and the outbreak of the war led to the publication of an American edition with a recommendation by General Winfield Scott, one of this country's greatest generals. The most important military analysts studied at that time and later were Baron Antoine Henri Jomini (*Vie politique et militaire de Napoléon . . . ; Précis de l'art de la guerre*) and Karl von Clausewitz (*On War*). Both of them based their somewhat variant analyses on Napoleon's wars, or at least claimed to do so.

Marshal Ferdinand Foch, the Allied generalissimo in World War I, was an ardent disciple of Napoleon, as were at least some of his subordinates. When David Lloyd George, the British prime minister, visited General de Castelnau, the commanding officer of the Second French Army on the western front, he commented that it was larger than any army Napoleon had ever commanded in one battle. The general replied, "Ah, Napoleon, Napoleon. If he were here now, he'd have thought of something else."[3] In 1950 General Douglas MacArthur, at Inchon in Korea, prided himself on taking the North Koreans in the rear in the classical Napoleonic pattern.

[2] *Napoleon Bonaparte.* New York: Oxford University Press, 1952, p. 311.
[3] John Terraine, "Big Battalions: the Napoleonic Legacy." *History Today,* June 1962, p. 416.

DATES OF NAPOLEON'S FIGHTS WITH HIS MAJOR ENEMIES

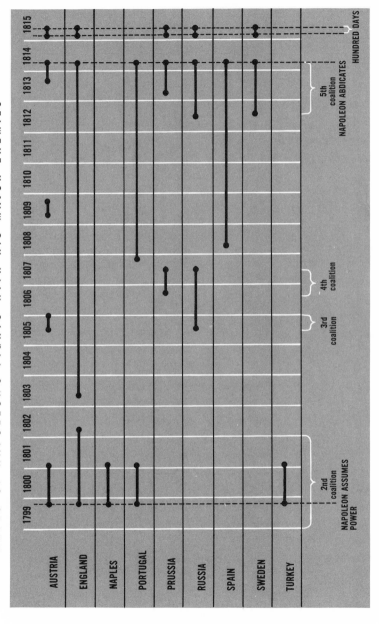

THE NAPOLEONIC REVOLUTION

Why this continued emulation of Napoleon? Not because he was a great military innovator, for he tended to be conservative. But he was the first to incorporate and apply all the principles devised by the military writers of the 18th century; later he extended them to larger operations than they had in mind. His mastery of the new military techniques is reflected in this quotation from a recent book:

In the controversies of the eighteenth century the military writers of France developed a system of tactics which, embodied finally in the Ordinance of 1791, consummated a long period of tactical improvement and played an important part in the triumphs of the wars which followed almost immediately. They evolved also doctrines of artillery employment and of strategy which were essential elements of Napoleon's art of war. . . . Napoleon alone clearly took advantage of all that was thus made available. Drawing from these varied sources, he welded them into a consistent practice far superior to any previously employed.[4]

In order to understand the wide variety of theoretical resources available to Napoleon, we must first remember the situation in the latter part of the 18th century. France had not fared well in the wars of the mid-century. It is natural for a losing country, rather than the victor, to think about military changes. Between the two world wars, for instance, Germany did more experimenting than did the western democracies. Similarly, the leaders of France prior to the French Revolution had ample motive for devising new military principles.

Another factor contributing to the large number of military essays produced in France at this time was the Enlightenment. France was the leader of this movement and the home of its most illustrious representatives. Their emphasis on reason was not limited to the natural and social sciences or the arts; writers on military affairs likewise attempted to exemplify the rationalism of the age.

[4] Robert S. Quimby, *The Background of Napoleonic Warfare.* New York: Columbia University Press, 1957, p. 344.

The military theorizing of the time is more easily understood if we realize that the latter part of the 18th century constituted a transitional military period, when most experts finally agreed that firepower was more important than the shock power of bayonet attacks. The champions of shock power were not quite so out-moded as they may seem from our 20th-century vantage point, for the musket of that day was slow-loading and had a limited range. (Its effective range was less than two hundred yards, and four shots in three minutes was considered a good average.) But upon the decision as to which method was the more important depended the decision of what tactics should be used. A column obviously had more shock power than a line, but a line could deliver much more effective firepower.

Four of the French theorists especially influenced Napoleon. The earliest was Marshal Maurice de Saxe (1696–1750), whose *Mes rêveries* advocated, among other things, relentless pursuit of a defeated enemy to complete the victory won on the battlefield. His idea that the ground often gave opportunities the enemy had overlooked in making his dispositions, Napoleon applied to the wider sphere of a theater of war. From General Pierre de Bourcet (1700–80) Napoleon learned a good deal about the use of massed artillery. Baron Joseph Du Teil (1723–94), of whom Napoleon was at one time a favorite pupil, laid down principles for mountain fighting. Napoleon later stated what he had learned: "Skill in . . . [mountain] warfare consists in occupying positions on the flanks or in the rear of the enemy, leaving him no alternative other than to abandon his positions without fighting in order to take up others in the rear, or to come out from them in order to attack you."[5]

[5] The sources of quotations from Napoleon are identified in footnotes if in copyright. The author of the present volume is responsible for the translations of all quotations not already available in English. Napoleon's maxims quoted on the following pages are taken from Conrad H. Lanza (ed.), *Napoleon and Modern War*. Harrisburg, Pa., 1949, passim.

The most advanced of these writers on military theory was Jacques de Guibert (1743–1790), author of an *Essai général de tactique.*[6]

Points agreed on by most of the writers were incorporated into the Ordinance of 1791 for infantry. This ordinance was the basis of infantry tactics (*tactics* being that branch of military science and art which deals with disposing and maneuvering forces after close contact has been established with the enemy) during the wars of the French Revolution and the Napoleonic period. It provided for a "mixed order," calling for marching in column up to the attack, since columns were much more maneuverable than lines, and then swinging into a flexible alternation of columns and three-rank lines. Thus it represented a compromise between the champions of the two sides. The ordinance allowed leeway, recognizing that the terrain might demand tactics different from those normally prescribed. It also placed reliance on the *élan* of the French troops; but this was not a radical innovation, as writer after writer in the 18th century had found more spirit in the French troops than in their enemies.

The conception of the cavalry's role also changed in the latter part of the 18th century. The cavalry came to be considered purely a shock weapon rather than another armed force. In order to fulfill its new role, it had to depend on speed; to attain the desired swiftness required relatively more attention to quality and less to quantity.

It was also in the 18th century that artillery received an independent status. By the end of the century military men realized that artillery should be concentrated against a decisive point in the enemy's position, either that from which he might attack, or the one where he was most vulnerable to attack. The French had

[6] Guibert was also the prophet of Napoleon's coming. He predicted a state akin to republican Rome, which would almost inevitably lead to the rise of a great genius who would first assume dictatorial powers and then a throne and completely reform the military and political system.

made their artillery more mobile than that of any other country.

When Napoleon put into practice this fund of experience and expert theory, the mixed order, calling for a combination of shock- and fire-power, remained his favorite tactical organization. Although he grumbled for years about the uselessness of the third rank, he waited until the battle of Leipzig in 1813 before eliminating it and using a two-line front to obtain maximum fire-power. At least in the early years he relied heavily on skirmishers to keep the enemy off-balance so his own troops could arrange their battle formations; later, when the recruits were no longer so well trained, he relied on preparatory artillery fire. Basically, however, he was interested in strategy—the science and art of using time and space to meet the enemy under advantageous conditions—and he excelled in getting his men to the decisive place at the right time. He drove home the necessity of advance planning to achieve desired results:

A consecutive series of great actions is never the result of chance and luck; it is always the product of planning and genius.

A plan of campaign should take into consideration everything the enemy can do and prescribe the necessary measures to counteract him. Plans of campaign may be modified ad infinitum according to circumstances, the genius of the commander, the character of the troops, and the topography of the theater of war.

To Napoleon the entire aim of the tactical changes had been to gain greater mobility and maneuverability: "The strength of an army, like power in mechanics, is the product of the mass by the velocity. A rapid march augments the morale of an army, and increases its means of victory." He was inspired with the idea of mobility, which enabled him repeatedly to surprise his enemies. "War is composed of nothing but surprises. While a general should adhere to general principles, he should never lose the opportunity to profit by these surprises." This point he stressed in all his early and successful campaigns. When he marched against the Austrian general Karl Mack at Ulm in the fall of 1805, he reached his goal in less than half the time Mack thought it would take the French to move from the English Channel.

Napoleon's campaigns were the early versions of the 20th-century blitzkrieg, or lightning warfare. He tried to operate on interior lines so as to be able, by having less distance to move, to strike anywhere along the line, and even to maneuver into the enemy's rear and sever his line of communications. Napoleon was a master of diversions to feint the enemy out of position. One reason for his practice of living off the country was to avoid being bound to magazines (depots of military supplies) as 17th- and 18th-century generals had been; traveling light, his army could travel fast. This practice had its weaknesses: it was most suitable to a fertile area, and it demanded a short campaign. But only with him was a system of mobile warfare fully realized.

The speed with which Napoleon moved permitted him to gain the advantage in several ways. He was interested in enveloping the enemy, much as the pincers attacks of World War II attempted this same maneuver. Speed of movement also permitted him on many occasions to turn the enemy's flank; doing so was one of his aims, for the flank is always more vulnerable than the front, and an attack on it tends to cause confusion among troops on the defensive. Napoleon also chose, whenever possible, a point of attack which would divide the enemy forces, who were often from different states; the fact that he was fighting against a coalition frequently made his task easier. He could also concentrate his own forces before the enemy was able to take the same step and before making contact with his opponent. "A union of various bodies must never be made near the enemy, because the enemy by concentrating his forces may not only prevent their junction but may beat them separately." Because of his ability to move and strike swiftly, Napoleon dared to disperse his troops in the knowledge that he could reunite them when necessary. Conversely, dispersion of the divisions permitted greater mobility.

Napoleon's dispersion of his troops came from the realization, which he was the first to hold, that divisions were large enough to be self-sufficient. During the French Revolution and Napoleonic period, armies became larger. Divisions—and after 1800, corps—replaced regiments as the major unit. After 1805 even the corps had a full complement only of infantry; engineers joined the cavalry and heavy guns in a central reserve. As a concomitant of self-sufficiency, Napoleon granted corps commanders a greater degree of freedom than under earlier commanders or under Wellington. This self-sufficiency meant that divisions could be dispersed and still be supporting one another. Brigades could be shifted from division to division as needed. The rules of support which others, such as the writers, had glimpsed only for divisional purposes Napoleon extended to an entire theater—just as he did the rules for the use of terrain.

These are the main values for the military student today—to see how highly mobile units of moderate size but powerfully armed were able to operate independently. Napoleon was the first to grasp the principles of organized dispersion and apply them in a way permitting concentration when that was desirable.

Interested in mobility, Napoleon did not concern himself overmuch about his line of communications with France. But the line of operations, extending from the front to the city serving temporarily for the direction of rear operations, did vitally concern him: "An army must have but one line of operations. This must be maintained with care and abandoned only for major reasons."

Which of Napoleon's battles and campaigns are most studied for positive rather than negative reasons? First comes the Italian campaign of 1796–97, in which he cleverly separated the Sardinian and Austrian forces and attacked them in the rear. The Austerlitz campaign revealed in masterly fashion how to utilize and move inferior numbers so as to have superiority at the decisive points. The pursuit of the Prussians after Jena is classic;

in three weeks the French captured 140,000 prisoners and virtually wiped out the Prussian army. Friedland revealed Napoleon's ability to seize the advantage on ground with which he was not familiar. And in the 1814 campaign in France he exploited in masterly fashion the interior lines of communication.

Napoleon was in several respects a forerunner of the 20th-century world wars. He used the artillery to prepare the way for infantry attacks. He demanded fire superiority, as the writers had stressed, in order not to be disorganized or destroyed by the enemy's fire before reaching the enemy. Unlike his predecessors, he did not preach the conservation of ammunition, especially not for the artillery. He complained that the artillery did not fire enough—that it should fire continuously without calculating expenditure. He tried to give the guns enough rounds, approximately three hundred, for two battles, and the field commanders were expected to use these to the best possible advantage. At Toulon in 1793 Bonaparte employed massed artillery for siege purposes with great effectiveness. Yet it was not until 1808 that he used mass artillery on the battlefield. In part the delay resulted from the fact that in the early campaigns his armies were so superior in quality and his tactics and strategy so surpassed his enemies' that he did not need to place such reliance on artillery.

He anticipated the World War II idea of a theater commander. "Nothing is more important in war than unity of command. Thus, when war is waged against a single power, there must be but one army, acting on one line and led by one chief." As early as May 1796 he wrote the Directory from Italy after receiving a letter urging that he turn south and leave an army under Kellermann around Milan:

If you weaken your power by dividing your forces, . . . you will lose the finest opportunity to impose your rule in Italy. Everyone has his own method of waging war. General Kellermann has more experience and would do better than I, but the two of us together would do very badly.[7]

In Paris, Bonaparte told the Directory early in 1798 that "The whole of the navy situated in the area of the Army of England must, like the other arms, be entirely in the hands of the general commanding the Army."[8]

Napoleon realized more clearly than anybody before him the decisive importance of the type of arms used.

The tactics of modern armies is founded upon two principles: 1st, that they ought to occupy a front which permits them to put all their missile weapons in action with advantage; 2nd, that they ought to prefer above everything the advantage of occupying positions which dominate, prolong, enfilade the enemy lines, to the advantage of being covered by a ditch, a parapet or any other example of field works.

The nature of the arms decides the composition of the armies, of the plans of campaign, of marches, of positions, of camping, of orders of battle, of the outline and profile of fortified places.

Wars now differed from earlier, pre-Revolutionary ones in that they were ideological (initially on the side of the French, later on both sides), instead of being governmental, fought for limited political or military objectives, as had been the case in the 18th century. This meant several things. The Revolutionary soldiers now tried to destroy the enemy's army, rather than merely outmaneuver him and take prisoners. The new type of warfare involved the entire population rather than mercenaries or those unfortunate elements of the population who might be impressed into service.

The French Revolution saw a *levée en masse,* a conscription of all resources and making all elements of the population liable for

[7] Vincent J. Esposito and John Robert Elting, *A Military History and Atlas of the Napoleonic Wars.* New York: Frederick A. Praeger, 1964. Map 11.

[8] John Eldred Howard, *Letters and Documents of Napoleon.* New York: Oxford University Press, 1961. Vol. I, p. 226. The Army of England was the French army whose assigned task was the invasion of England.

service. In the Year VI (1798) the Directory passed a draft law for men aged twenty to twenty-five; it exempted married men, divorced men who were heads of families, and widowers. Conscription did not work very well during the Revolution; only one third of the conscripts ever reported. Bonaparte put teeth into the draft laws and made them work. From 1799 through 1805 2,000,000 were classed for conscription, and 1,250,000 called up. One fourth of all those called were rejected on physical grounds; Napoleon exempted those who supported families, and after the promulgation of the Concordat with the Papacy in 1802 exempted seminarians. The number actually serving reached 700,-000. In 1805 he replaced the local draft boards with prefects and subprefects, and by 1807 almost 100 per cent of the desired number of recruits reached the army. One reason is that Napoleon permitted draftees to obtain substitutes; as the campaigns became more dangerous, the price rose, until in 1812 it was 15,000 francs, ten times as high as in 1805.[9]

Although his demands, particularly after 1812, were heavy, Napoleon recruited within the 1789 borders of France only 2.1 million men in all the years he was in power. This figure did not represent a debilitating effect on the post-Napoleonic French male population; the population of France showed a considerable rise, in part because the draft led to early marriages. Ironically, his last army, in 1815, broke with the Revolutionary tradition Napoleon had inherited and followed. He was afraid to resort to conscription, or even to amalgamate the national guard and the regular army.

Napoleon differed from earlier generals in his success at raising, organizing, and equipping mass armies. These armies were made possible first of all by the improved roads of the 18th century; the better roads had been used initially, however, merely to transport more baggage per soldier rather than larger

[9] In 1812 and 1813 half the eligible men escaped serving in the army.

armies and heavier equipment such as guns. Secondly, even though Napoleon's factories were not capable of producing enough guns to build up a satisfactory reserve supply, the industrial revolution made it possible to turn out the vast numbers of items needed by a mass army. With it we have the start of modern war.

For what kind of innovations should Napoleon be given credit? First, for making propaganda a regular arm of the military. He clearly recognized the importance of morale. We shall see later the steps he took to maintain morale in the army with his orders of the day and his speeches to the assembled soldiers. His propaganda may be called a fourth kind of warfare, added to land, naval, and economic. Yet he recognized its limitations. "A good general, a good corps of officers, good organization, good training, rigid discipline make good troops, independent of the cause for which they fight." He discounted the value of speeches before a battle, saying the old soldiers did not listen and the recruits forgot them at the first cannon shot. Innuendo and false rumors should be destroyed, however, by the orders of the day.

In 1803 he organized the cavalry along lines that persisted as long as cavalry itself: light cavalry, dragoons, and heavy or battle cavalry. All these types were armed, and the cavalry had its own artillery. Napoleon's use of cavalry was masterful. In addition to the customary use for reconnaissance and pursuit, Napoleon employed it in all phases of battle. The cavalry screen was a new invention in 1805. The campaign of 1806 saw a new order of march, which Napoleon called the "squared battalion"; it was an attempt to approach the enemy by three parallel roads, with a cavalry screen across the entire front. Most of the cavalry was in independent units; Napoleon took the small formations of cavalry away from the divisions and united them into a corps. And he effected a co-ordination of the three major branches of the fighting forces: the infantry, the cavalry, and the artillery.

Several of Napoleon's most important military reforms concerned the artillery, at which he was expert. Even before Napoleon's day the artillery had interchangeable parts in the guns, carriages, and ammunition wagons. Napoleon standardized on a few gun calibers throughout the service. Formerly civilians had contracted to haul the guns to the battlefield, after which they had taken the horses away. This meant that the soldiers were forced to manhandle the guns if any moving was to be done during a battle. Napoleon eliminated this grievous system by including artillery horses on the regular table of supplies of the army. Auguste Marmont, who became one of Napoleon's marshals, was responsible for concentrating all the field guns under the division commander instead of scattering them throughout the battalions. Artillery was held in reserve at the disposal of the supreme commander.

Bonaparte was also the first to heed the admonition to have adequate reserves and use them intelligently. The formation of the Army of Reserve for the campaign of 1800 proved to be the decisive factor in defeating the Austrians, who could not believe that such an army actually existed.

Napoleon realized that war is not a science, but an art. "Nothing is absolute in war." For this reason Napoleon stated, "A general should say to himself many times a day: If the hostile army were to make its appearance on my front, on my right, or on my left, what should I do?" . . . "In everything that is undertaken, two thirds must be calculated and one third left to chance. To increase the first fraction would be pusillanimous; to augment the second would be rash." Himself an avid student of the campaigns of great captains, from Alexander to Frederick, Napoleon believed that "knowledge of grand tactics is gained only by experience and by the study of the history of the campaigns of all the great captains."

Yet warfare is based on principles and scientific knowledge. "All great captains have accomplished great things only by conforming to the rules and natural principles of the art of war." . . .

"War should be made methodically, for it should have a definite object; and it should be conducted according to the principles and rules of the art. War should be made with forces proportionate to the obstacles which can be foreseen."

Being a successful general involved having certain personal qualities. Marshal Saxe said that the three basic qualities of a good general are courage, without which nothing else avails; intelligence, which should be courageous and "fertile in expedients"; and health. Napoleon's definition was strikingly similar:

It is exceptional and difficult to find in one man all the qualities necessary for a great general. That which is most desirable and which instantly sets a man apart, is that his intelligence or talent be balanced by his character or courage. If his courage is the greater, a general heedlessly undertakes things beyond his ability. If on the contrary his character or courage is less than his intelligence he does not dare carry out his plans.

Napoleon shone particularly as a field commander. The qualities that go to make up such a man are elusive; Napoleon thought a person was born with them. Among them are an ability to appraise the situation rapidly and accurately (for example, foreseeing developments merely by noting campfires on the eve of a battle); selecting exactly the right moment to take offensive action;[10] understanding the psychology both of one's men and of the enemy commander. These items all fall under the rubric of military art rather than military science; if one could learn the clue to how he inspired his men, the effort put into the study would be well rewarded.

Although there is no question that Napoleon was a genius as a field commander, he did have important weaknesses. Some were caused by youthful inexperience; but most of them appeared in the last half-dozen years of his reign. The later ones

[10] Bonaparte wrote: "The fate of a battle is a question of a single moment, a single thought; . . . the decisive moment arrives, the moral spark is kindled, and the smallest reserve force settles the matter."

did not surprise Napoleon, for in 1805 he said, "A man has his day in war as in other things; I myself shall be good for it another six years, after which I shall have to stop."

He did not effect necessary or desirable changes so rapidly as he might—for example, the use of massed artillery—and he rejected such new tools of warfare as the balloon. In 1799 he abolished the French Balloon Corps, formed five years before. Although medical officers and regimental aid stations moved forward with the troops, and although Bonaparte came to realize the importance of sanitation while in Italy, he did not change the system inherited from the Directory of disbanding the physicians and surgeons in time of peace, for reasons of economy.

In the Iberian Peninsula Napoleon was never able to adapt his method of fighting to the guerrilla warfare. He erred first in not making careful plans for the campaign in Spain. There he relied on the methods used in Egypt, which had proved effective in Naples and in the Vendée. He used columns, not suited for this type of warfare, too extensively. To combat guerrilla resistance effectively, Napoleon would have needed a force strong enough to occupy all the essential points, cover his communications, and still have enough troops left to range the countryside to destroy the enemy. Raw recruits constituted too large a proportion, almost 60 per cent, of the army in Spain. Yet it was less Napoleon's mistakes than Wellington's army that represented the difference between success and failure in the French attempt to bring the Spanish guerrillas to heel.

Once he recognized that the quality of his army was deteriorating, particularly after the breakup of his first Grand Army in order to provide troops for Spain in 1808, Napoleon tended to rely increasingly on masses of soldiers. He did not recognize that there is a maximum optimum size for an army. Use of massive formations was most evident in the Russian campaign of 1812, which he undertook with about 600,000 men, by far the largest army seen in modern times until then. The very size of this force deprived it of that mobility which he constantly preached and which had won him so many victories, and he lost touch with the main Russian armies. Significantly, he fell back on the logistical system of magazines. His numerical strength further meant that the Russians were not willing to offer battle; Napoleon therefore had to pursue them for 600 miles.[11] When he finally caught them at Borodino, he violated some of his other precepts: "Generals who keep troops fresh for the day after the battle are almost always defeated. If it may usefully be done, they should expend the last man, because on the day after a complete success there is no obstacle before them." Napoleon failed to display the courage, the character as he called it, of a great general to make the necessary decisions; he would not commit his Guard to make the victory decisive because he thought he was too far from home to run the risk. As he himself said, "He who wishes to make quite sure of everything in war, and never ventures, will always be at a disadvantage. . . . Boldness is the acme of wisdom." He further broke with his own teaching and practice at Borodino by ordering a frontal attack which was bound to be costly.

The maxims of Napoleon referred to above were not collected as such and published by him. They were rather statements written by him at various times and in diverse places, and then excerpted for whatever they might teach later students of military science and art. Most of the lessons are still valid today.

The validity of his theories of warfare is perhaps shown by the fact that he lost when he disregarded them. Reference has already been made to the Russian campaign. In 1813 Napoleon made the mistake of tying himself for the first time to fortresses,

---

[11] It is worth noting that there was no conscious plan on the part of the Russians to weaken the French by drawing them farther into Russia. The Russian generals retreated because they did not dare to stand and fight. Napoleon himself, between a thousand and fifteen hundred miles from home, was far more cautious than he had ever been.

thus reducing his freedom of movement. On the eve of Waterloo he dispatched Marshal Emmanuel Grouchy to watch General Gebhard von Blücher despite his maxims: "No detachment should be made on the eve of a battle, because conditions may change during the night." . . . "When a commander intends to give battle, he should collect all his forces and overlook none; a battalion sometimes decides the day."

With Napoleon, if not with the wars of the French Revolution, modern war begins. Yet the development of modern war has probably been based on a misconception of Napoleon's thinking, especially as viewed by Clausewitz, who is considered the foremost interpreter of Napoleon. Clausewitz made military theory of the 19th and early 20th centuries look to the legend of Napoleon's mass victories rather than to earlier triumphs won by movement and surprise. Actually, Napoleon resorted to use of numbers only when the quality of his infantry declined because of lack of training and the injection of foreign troops; this reliance on numbers characterized the decline of his military prowess. Napoleon at first thought in terms of *potential* unity of forces; Clausewitz insisted on *physical concentration* of forces. Translated into modern war, this emphasis on numbers became the trench warfare and useless slaughter of World War I. The British (for example, General Douglas Haig, commander-in-chief in World War I) blindly accepted Clausewitz because they thought he was the apostle of Napoleon. Another erring disciple of Napoleon was Colonel de Grandmaison, Foch's prize pupil, perhaps led astray by other maxims of Napoleon:

The man who cannot look upon a battlefield dry-eyed will allow many men to be killed uselessly.

The first object which a general who gives battle should consider is the glory and honor of his arms; the safety and consideration of his men is but secondary; but it is also true that in audacity and obstinacy will be found the safety and conservation of the men.

Disregarding Napoleon's idea of winning with the lowest possible cost in human life, Grandmaison stressed pushing the offensive to the extreme, even though this inevitably involved "bloody sacrifice." He advocated use of the bayonet, for shock effect, despite the great development of firepower since the 18th century, when the supremacy of firepower over shock was already accepted.

Jomini was another who passed on a misconception of Napoleon's strategy, stressing the effect of mass rather than surprise. He further thought in terms of the single objective, rather than of one that offered alternatives. This from a man who, in discussing the later phase of Napoleon's actions, wrote, "One might say that he was sent into this world to teach generals and statesmen what they ought to avoid."

Napoleon's military career would have guaranteed his memory, even if it had been his only accomplishment. One author has written:

> So long as military men survive, until every sword is beaten back into a ploughshare, the name of Napoleon will be respected by those who follow and study the profession of arms. Jurists may think of his code, publicists of his civic programs, nationalists of the way in which he recreated the patriotism of France, democrats of the way he rescued the principles of free government which the mobilized monarchs of Europe were avid to destroy. But even though these others might fail him in appreciation and ultimately deplore and discount his contributions, the soldiers of the world will still render him homage.[12]

It was Napoleon's military successes which gave rise to the reform of the Prussian army, one of the important results of his reign. A few of the Prussian military leaders had realized even before the battle of Jena that the army of Frederick the Great no longer sufficed to maintain Prussia's position, but it was the

---

[12] Elbridge Colby, *Masters of Mobile Warfare.* Princeton, N.J.: Princeton University Press, 1943, p. 105.

debacle of 1806 that enabled the reformers to effect some changes.

Most of the recommendations came from a Military Reorganization Commission. It functioned until a Ministry of War, created in December of 1808, gave a unified administration to military affairs for the first time. A basic defect of the pre-1806 Prussian army had been that its battalions or regiments fought by themselves; under the reform program, brigades were organized and units were trained to fight in co-operation with other arms of the service. The brigade also became the unit of supply under a Central War Commissariat; far better accounting systems were introduced, and captains and colonels now lost the profit earlier obtained by selling supply items to their men. The system of furloughing men to work as artisans during peacetime also came to an end. (Their pay had gone to their commanding officers.) Foreign recruiting was stopped. Military justice, under new Articles of War, was mitigated, so that running the gauntlet, for example, was eliminated.

Several steps were taken to improve the caliber of officers. Non-aristocrats could now become officers, though in practice few did. Officers had to pass an examination to obtain a commission or a promotion. Three new military schools were founded, Cadet Institutes with a five-year course of study established, and a special three-year course instituted for fifty advanced officers. All of this military education was co-ordinated.

Gerhard von Scharnhorst was the leading light in this military reform. In addition to the administrative reorganization he also revamped Prussian army tactics, in many respects imitating those of the French—complete reconnaissance, attacking in columns, use of sharpshooters. Scharnhorst was able to effect these reforms largely because of the support of Freiherr vom und zum Stein, who was the leading minister until Napoleon demanded his dismissal in 1808.

Neither Scharnhorst nor Stein had been able to obtain during

Prussia's reform period from 1807 to 1813 the most basic military reform they sought, one which could overcome the differential existing between the French and other European armies ever since the days of the Revolution. That vainly desired change was the formation of a national army, based on conscription free of a class basis, rather than the professional and peasant army Prussia and other states had. (Austria did adopt conscription in 1809.) The military conservatives, and especially the king, feared the impact of such a changed military concept on the social and political setup of the state. In 1813, however, after Prussia had split from Napoleon and gone to war against him, it was necessary to enlarge the army rapidly. This was done by relying on a Landwehr, or militia, first in East Prussia and then throughout the kingdom, by decree of March 17.[13] In East Prussia all men between the ages of eighteen and forty-five were subject to service in the Landwehr; in the kingdom at large, the ages were seventeen to forty, without substitution. In 1813 the Landwehr had 120,000 men. In the Leipzig campaign, the last big battle in the War of Liberation, the Prussian forces were one-third regular army, one-third reservist, and one-third Landwehr. Scharnhorst thought the East Prussian plan did not go far enough, for it permitted substitutes and stated that the Landwehr would serve only in the province of East Prussia. In a decree of February 9, 1813, concerning conscription in the regular army for the duration of the war, Scharnhorst had committed himself to a policy of no exemptions and no substitutions.

Plans were also laid for a Landsturm, composed of all those incapable of more active service, for a last-ditch defense of their home districts. (That extremist nationalist, Adolf Hitler, resorted

[13] Until recently historians thought that Prussia was able to put a large army into the field against Napoleon in 1813 because of the *Krümper* system of short-term training for civilians. In actuality this system, which had been in effect for furlough reasons long before the debacle of 1806, produced only 35,000 men.

to the same steps as last-ditch defense measures in World War II.) The Landsturm was proclaimed by royal decree on April 21, 1813. In its original form, however, it lasted only three months, in large part because of protests against its leveling tendencies. All able-bodied men between the ages of fifteen and sixty were put on its rolls. In July a decree that placed limitations on and allowed exceptions to the universal obligation of service crippled the spontaneous enthusiasm which was the main justification of the Landsturm.

In the spring of 1814, after the capture of Paris, the king ordered reinstatement of the old exemptions from military service. It was only on September 3, 1814, that Prussia finally obtained obligatory military service, by a law which dealt with all branches of the armed forces. Men between the ages of twenty and twenty-five were subject to being drafted for three years of army service. The first reserve Landwehr was composed of men in the twenty to twenty-five age group who were not drafted, plus all men from twenty-six to thirty-two. The second reserve Landwehr consisted of veterans of the regular army and first reserve plus all others under forty. The age limits of the Landsturm, to include all men not serving in any other military units, were seventeen and fifty. On November 11, 1815, a decree detailed regulations for the Landwehr, which was to be a local institution in each district.

A national army was possible in Prussia at this particular time because the country was no longer under Napoleon's thumb. Knowing how much more effective a national army based on the principle of universal service could be, Napoleon would not have permitted it.

Prussia's military system had now caught up with the French. It may have passed the latter, because Prussia's far smaller population of five million led the authorities to apply the *levée en masse* with greater rigor than was the case in France. Henceforth, except for England, European armies were national, or citizen, armies. This factor was the most significant of all reforms made by other countries in their efforts to match Napoleon's success in warfare. What France had begun, the other states could ignore only at their peril.

But while Napoleon unquestionably set the pace for land warfare, his knowledge of naval warfare was just as unquestionably inadequate. He realized that it took longer to train seamen than to train soldiers, but—like Joseph Stalin in the 20th century—he never appreciated the difference between the two types of forces. His concept of an admiral is almost ludicrous: "On the sea nothing is genius or inspiration; everything is positive and empiric. The admiral needs only one science, that of navigation. . . . An admiral needs to divine nothing; he knows where the enemy is and his strength."

Yet Napoleon recognized the importance of naval warfare, and he never gave up. He built ships modeled on the best available, and ship for ship they were better than the English. The French officers and crews could not compare, however, with the British. Although the battle of Trafalgar established British naval supremacy, Napoleon continued squadron warfare against Britain, raiding its lines of communications and its colonies, until 1809, when the Spanish revolt ended these French efforts. The Spanish colonies, which had served as bases for the French, now turned against them. As early as 1811 the London *Courier* stated, "The sea is ours, and we must maintain the doctrine—that no nation, no fleet, no cockboat shall sail upon it without our permission."

Napoleon also tried a third method of warfare—economic. He was forced to it by the fact that his most consistent and major opponent was Great Britain. As he was master of the land, Britain was master of the sea—particularly after Trafalgar, so disastrous to the French. The two giants, like the elephant and the whale, were unable to get at each other in direct combat. All that the British fleet could do in Europe was land troops at a suitable spot; though this forced Napoleon to guard his entire coastline, it was never decisive.

Even before the time of Napoleon, during the Seven Years'

War (1756–63) and the French Revolution, the two countries had waged economic warfare against each other. But Napoleon was the first to try to organize it into a project as vast as the Continental System, designed, as he wrote, "to conquer the sea by power of the land." The System itself began with the issuance in November 1806 of the Berlin Decree, in retaliation for Britain's having declared the entire coast of Europe from the Elbe River to Brest in a state of blockade. Napoleon issued his decree just after having defeated the Prussian army, and while on his way eastward to deal with the Russian army, the last remaining major opponent on the Continent. He claimed, and the British in essence acknowledged, that the British blockade was a paper blockade, one they could not enforce along the entire coast. The British had indicated that they would enforce it absolutely only between Ostend and Brest. After claiming that the British blockade was illegal because it could not be enforced, Napoleon was declaring a blockade, of even poorer quality paper, of the British Isles. The Berlin Decree in addition forbade those parts of Europe under French control to buy English goods or goods carried in British ships.

The government of England retaliated in 1807 with some orders in council (decrees issued by the Cabinet—theoretically by the monarch—without prior consultation with Parliament). These forbade neutrals to sail to the Continent without first having touched in England to have their cargoes examined and to obtain a license to proceed. They constituted an extension of the Rule of 1756 to coastal shipping between enemy ports from which English ships were excluded. The Rule had stated initially that trade prohibited in peacetime could not be opened in time of war. Britain realized it could not starve out France or end the Continent's warlike industries, but it expected to profit materially by the blockade.

In the Milan Decree at the end of 1807, Napoleon declared that any ship complying with these British rules would be considered denationalized and therefore subject to seizure as a pirate ship.

Further decrees followed. Napoleon had not been able to stop smuggling, so the Fontainebleau Decree of October 18, 1810, ordered the seizure and burning of any British goods found on the Continent. After the United States imposed an embargo during Jefferson's presidency, Napoleon declared that since all American ships were off the seas, any claiming to be American were lawful prize and should be sequestered. By the Rambouillet Decree of March 23, 1810, he ordered them sold with their cargoes.

In adopting the type of economic warfare on which he embarked, Napoleon was influenced by mercantilistic and physiocratic, as well as by pragmatic, considerations. The blockade was physiocratic to the extent that Napoleon believed the Continent would be able to withstand economic warfare better than England since it was obviously better endowed with natural resources. As early as the time of his youthful garrison duty at Auxonne, Bonaparte had concluded from his study of history that an agricultural, military state would almost always defeat a commercial, maritime, naval state. What he overlooked was the fact that England was also largely self-supporting. Napoleon's theories were mercantilistic to the extent that he believed a country needed a favorable balance of trade—and of no country was this more true than of England, a "nation of shopkeepers." Napoleon thought he could provoke bankruptcy, unemployment, surrender, and perhaps revolution.

Neither side, in its economic warfare, necessarily advocated a cessation of trade with the other; but England wanted to keep the trade in its own hands and to export more than it bought, while Napoleon wanted the trade to be exclusively an export trade to Britain. The Continental System was, then, a boycott rather than a blockade.

From the pragmatic rather than theoretical point of view, Napoleon was prompted to set up the Continental System not only by a desire to retaliate against specific British measures (and deciding who was retaliating against whom is a difficult problem), but also by his analysis of how to overcome a hostile England. Britain, through its credit, its head start in industrialization, and its commercial leadership, was able to subsidize each of the members of every coalition, and to hold out hopes of such subsidies to obtain allies. If its commercial source of income could be cut off, the British would be unable to make payments to real or potential allies. British producers, unable to sell their products, would become dissatisfied with the government's policy; unemployed workers might actually revolt against their rulers. Britain, after first discontinuing aid to Continental powers, would eventually have to make peace with Napoleon and the Continent.

In order for the system to work, Napoleon had to close off the entire Continent to British goods. By the Treaty of Tilsit, Russia agreed to join the System. Prussia was forced to close its ports to British shipping. France and Russia also agreed that if Sweden did not join, Russia might go to war with it and seize Finland as compensation. This is what happened.

After Tilsit Napoleon tried to stop the importation of British goods by Portugal, "England's oldest ally." In order to reach it, Napoleon's army had to go through Spain. Thus began that peninsular war which between the years 1808 and 1813 drained away manpower needed for other military operations.

Napoleon never was able to enforce the Continental System. It wounded so many interests—producers, merchants, consumers—that virtually everybody was seeking to circumvent it. Strict enforcement required military occupation. Contraband flourished, perhaps as at no other time, especially when Napoleon had to use his troops on campaign.

Yet developments showed that the blockade had great potentialities for harming England. British exports declined drastically between 1806 and 1808. Exports of British goods to northern

Europe in 1808 were a little over a fifth (20.9 per cent) of what they had been in 1805, and British re-exports a little over half (51.6 per cent). The boycott certainly contributed to, and may actually have caused, the severe depression of 1810 in Britain. In 1811 British commerce fell by about a sixth, in part because Sweden had joined the boycott. If the System had been rigorously applied for a long period of time, it might have brought John Bull to his knees, provided Napoleon could have got the United States to shut off its commerce with England.

Four factors saved Britain. The United States continued to trade with it, although on a much-reduced scale in 1811, after the adoption of a nonintercourse policy by the United States. British exports to the United States rose again in 1812 prior to the outbreak of war in June.

A second factor was the opening of trade with Latin America. Although the Americas did not buy as much as the British had expected, in part because of old regulations and in part because of the civil wars starting in 1810, the trade with Latin America greatly reduced the pressure of the System on Britain. British sales to America exclusive of the United States rose from £8 million in 1805 to almost £20 million in 1808 and 1809. Latin America's imports from Great Britain in 1812 were seventeen times what they had been in 1802.

Furthermore, the effectiveness of the blockade depended upon Napoleon's being consistently victorious. Less than two years after his last territorial extension to enforce his System he was meeting defeat in the vastness of Russia.

Lastly, Napoleon vitiated his own System. The St. Cloud Decree of July 3, 1810, regularized the granting of licenses to carry on trade otherwise forbidden. By the Trianon Tariff of August 5, 1810, Napoleon admitted colonial wares even of enemy origin upon payment of a 50 per cent ad valorem tariff. In effect, he became his own smuggler. This new approach weakened the whole project, for people thought Napoleon was getting ready to renounce the System after having erred in inaugurating it. Napoleon made this blunder in part because of the System's unpopularity at home and because it was having an adverse effect on his customs revenue.[14]

The mercantilist side of his thinking led Napoleon so far astray that he sacrificed the opportunity to starve England out in 1810, after two consecutive bad harvests. Napoleon sold wheat to England at this time because his attention was focused on draining precious metals from his adversary, so it would no longer be able to subsidize Continental coalitions.

Napoleon further weakened the System by continuing to respect the international banking framework that supported British trade and facilitated the transfer of funds by which England subsidized the coalitions against him. In 1812 British exports rose again because Russia and Sweden were opened to them, and contraband could play a more important role in Germany after Napoleon moved his troops eastward. Napoleon had missed his great opportunity in 1811, when he controlled almost the entire Continent and Great Britain was suffering from crop failures.

Though it was the only feasible way Napoleon could get at England, the System was worse than a failure, it was a blunder. The positive aspect of it, in contrast to the negative anti-British facet, called for France to provide the items which the countries could no longer obtain from England. But France could not supply them. It could not get for Europe the colonial goods, such as sugar and coffee, which were so highly desired. (The demand for these was so strong that Napoleon issued the Trianon Tariff mentioned above and later complained that they were the items which defeated his purpose.) Nor could France furnish the manufactured goods the rest of the Continent wanted. In part it was

[14] The British also had to violate the principles stated in their 1807 Orders in Council. In April 1808 the Cabinet got from Parliament the right in specific cases to permit sailing for effectively blockaded ports and the exporting or importing of prohibited goods.

hampered by the tariffs of the various states. More fundamental, however, was the fact that despite Napoleon's encouragement, French industry was not sufficiently advanced to supply the Continent; even if it had been, the means of transportation were lacking. France could not safely carry on coastal shipping, and neither the roads nor the wagons and horses existed to carry the relatively vast amount of goods by land.

What were the results of the Continental System? For the long term, the most important was that it increased the gap between the British and Continental economies. Despite France's efforts to replace England as a supplier, the System slowed economic progress on the Continent more than in England.[15] It was England's fortune to have a capitalism sufficiently ahead of the other countries to give it a clear superiority without being so industrialized that it was totally dependent on imports for its subsistence. Although British capitalism was bruised by the Continental System, it came out of the battle more dynamic than ever, ready to conquer the world; because European markets seemed relatively less important now, the British turned more to the overseas potential. More immediately, the Continental System played an important part in bringing on the War of 1812.

Napoleon angered much of Europe by putting the interests of France (or himself) first. Pius VII's refusal to incorporate the Papal States in the Continental System led to a series of measures culminating in his arrest by the French: Napoleon declared himself sovereign over the Papal States; the Pope refused to acknowledge this action and excommunicated Napoleon; the French thereupon arrested him. Napoleon's treatment of Pius VII did much to strengthen and raise to fanatic proportions the opposition in Spain. The System was one of the major factors in losing him his most important ally, Russia. The Russian nobles had only recently, in the last twenty years, developed a profitable

[15] The Continental System also led to the establishment of new industries in France. These will be treated in Chapter V.

grain export trade with Britain; they resented the forced decline in their incomes. In December of 1810 Tsar Alexander, pressured by the only social class in Russia to which he paid heed, announced that he would no longer enforce the Continental System; henceforth he would admit previously banned goods, and he would levy a tariff on imports from France.

The System led Napoleon to annex additional territories—one of them, Oldenburg, belonged to a brother-in-law of Alexander I, and its annexation helped bring on the breach between the two Emperors. Also annexed with the aim of enforcing the Continental System were the Papal States, Holland, and northwest Germany. Their acquisition made Europe fearful of just how far-reaching Napoleon's ambition might be. Napoleon's activity as a manipulator of boundaries, therefore, sprang in part from the attempt to make the Continental System effective.

The realignment of the map of Europe resulted from all phases of Napoleon's wars. The Continental System was the economic front; in addition there were the naval and military fronts.

Napoleon began his rearrangement of the map of Europe seven years before he took the title of Emperor and two years before he assumed control of the government as First Consul. In the Treaty of Campoformio he began that process of cartography which eventually promoted the concept of Italian unity. Lombardy, Modena, and some of the Papal Legations were combined into a classically named Cisalpine Republic. Austria got Venetia, which never again became an independent state. After the Treaty of Lunéville the Cisalpine Republic was enlarged, and somewhat later it received the name of Italian Republic. When Bonaparte became Emperor, he obviously could not be president of a republic in Italy, so he had the name changed to Kingdom of Italy—a name with lasting implications. To this state Venetia was added in 1805.

The entire southern part of the peninsula was included in the

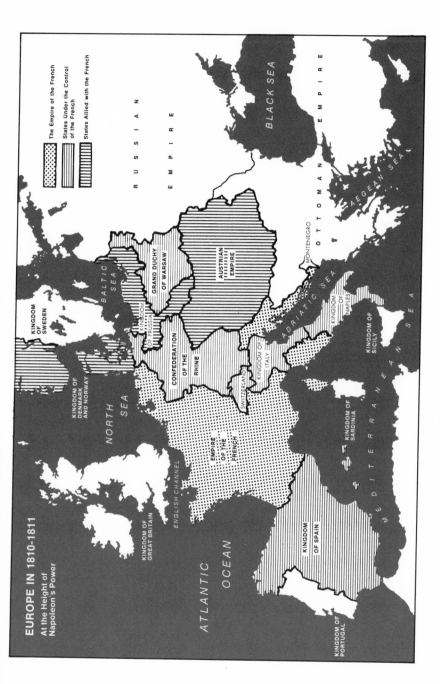

EUROPE IN 1810-1811
At the Height of Napoleon's Power

The Empire of the French

States Under the Control of the French

States Allied with the French

ATLANTIC OCEAN

KINGDOM OF GREAT BRITAIN

ENGLISH CHANNEL

KINGDOM OF PORTUGAL

KINGDOM OF SPAIN

EMPIRE OF THE FRENCH

NORTH SEA

KINGDOM OF DENMARK AND NORWAY

KINGDOM OF SWEDEN

BALTIC SEA

KINGDOM OF PRUSSIA

GRAND DUCHY OF WARSAW

CONFEDERATION OF THE RHINE

AUSTRIAN EMPIRE

RUSSIAN EMPIRE

SWITZERLAND

KINGDOM OF ITALY

ADRIATIC SEA

MONTENEGRO

OTTOMAN EMPIRE

KINGDOM OF SARDINIA

KINGDOM OF NAPLES

KINGDOM OF SICILY

MEDITERRANEAN SEA

AEGEAN SEA

BLACK SEA

Kingdom of Naples, over which first Joseph Bonaparte and then Napoleon's brother-in-law Joachim Murat reigned as king. Napoleon further wanted to establish a territorial link between the kingdoms of Italy and Naples. Most of the west coast of the Italian peninsula, down to and including the Papal States, was incorporated into the French Empire. The peninsula thus had only three parts as against the nine major and several minor states prior to the French Revolution. The Italian people now glimpsed the idea of a national, united state.

Napoleon's reduction in the number of German states had even greater import because the eventual unification of Germany precipitated a series of events leading to World War I. He never intended to create a one-state area, but he did want to reduce the number of German states so as to make the area more manageable.

Provision for such reduction had been made both in the Treaty of Basel with Prussia in 1795 and in the Treaty of Campoformio with Austria in 1797. But nothing happened until after the Treaty of Lunéville, in part because of the early outbreak of the War of the Second Coalition. Lunéville provided that France and Russia might supervise the reorganization of Germany; Russia actually had very little to say about it. The reorganization was made necessary by a clause that France would receive the left bank of the Rhine River, with the states losing territory to be indemnified by land on the right bank. It was quite obvious that the ecclesiastical states would be among those to go. As they had been one of the main supports of the Habsburg emperor, the Habsburgs would thereby be weakened.

The reorganization was agreed to in a document with the splendid if somewhat frightening name of *Reichsdeputationshauptschluss* (chief conclusion of the imperial deputation). So long as the number of German states was reduced, Bonaparte did not greatly care who got what; the actual decisions were largely left to Talleyrand, his foreign minister, who was not above being influenced by bribes. (Americans had made his acquaintance five years before in the XYZ affair.) All but six of the city-states of Germany disappeared (Augsburg, Bremen, Hamburg, Lübeck, Frankfurt, and Nürnberg). The church lost two and a half million subjects and over $10 million in annual revenue. Concomitantly, eighteen universities were secularized. Also swallowed up were the lands held by the free imperial knights. The princes in whose states the knights' lands were enclaves simply added this property to their own holdings. By the end of the Napoleonic period, the territory later incorporated in one united German state had only thirty-nine states instead of the more than three hundred and sixty (not counting the imperial knights) it had in 1789.

The Treaty of Pressburg, after the War of the Third Coalition in 1805, provided that the states which had aided Napoleon would gain territory—among them Bavaria, Württemberg, and Baden. In addition, the first two became kingdoms, and Baden moved up a step in rank to a grand duchy.

Even more importantly, the treaty provided for the establishment of a third state in Germany, a Confederation of the Rhine, which would take its place alongside Austria and Prussia, and whose members would no longer be in the Holy Roman Empire. Emperor Francis in Vienna, foreseeing what was going to happen, in 1804 had taken the title Emperor of Austria (formerly he had merely been grand duke of that state). In August of 1806 he proclaimed the end of the Holy Roman Empire, the thousand-year Reich, realizing that it had become meaningless.

By the Peace of Tilsit in 1807, Alexander of Russia agreed that Napoleon might establish a Duchy of Warsaw taken from the gains of Prussia in the second and third partitions of Poland in 1793 and 1795. After the Austrian war of 1809, Napoleon enlarged Warsaw with Galicia, gained by Austria in the first partition. The existence of a satellite Polish state helped keep alive, even after Napoleon's fall, the idea of an independent Poland.

THE NAPOLEONIC REVOLUTION

In at least one respect Napoleon kept the map of Europe from being changed. Russia had for centuries wanted a warm-water port or ports, and more recently had cast covetous eyes on Constantinople and the Straits. Though Napoleon's policy in the Near and Middle East was basically anti-Russian, at Tilsit he did offer freedom of the Straits to Russia. At that time Alexander agreed to evacuate the Danubian principalities, Moldavia and Wallachia, which Russia had invaded upon the outbreak of war with Turkey in 1806. The Treaty of Tilsit stated that Turkey should lose most of its Balkan provinces if it did not come to terms with Russia, but Napoleon wanted to await a general European peace before anything concrete was done or any more negotiations carried on. At Erfurt, where he tried to placate Alexander in 1808, Napoleon conceded that Russia might gain the two provinces and Bessarabia, and reluctantly stated that he would be willing to let Russia have Constantinople in return for continued alliance and friendship, on condition that France possess the Dardanelles. By the end of 1808 Alexander was demanding the Straits. On the matter of the Dardanelles Napoleon was adamant; and without the Dardanelles, Russia would still not have the access to the Mediterranean it wanted. Neither side would yield, and as a result Russia virtually abnegated its duties and obligations as an ally. More indicative of French policy than this talk about annexing various Turkish possessions were Napoleon's statement in 1806 that he would not favor partitioning the Ottoman Empire even if he got three fourths of it, and Talleyrand's directive that a major objective of French policy in the Eastern question "must be the closure of the Bosporus to the Russians, and the prohibition of the passage from the Mediterranean to the Black Sea of all their ships, whether armed or unarmed."

By his stand, Napoleon effectively checked Russia's advance in this area. By the time he was deposed, nationalism, as shown in a Serb revolt starting as early as 1804 and a Greek revolution starting in 1821, was a strong enough force to act as a check on

Russian ambitions. Napoleon's policies were imitated by later generations of Frenchmen, who insisted that Russia should be excluded from the Dardanelles. Russia did gain Bessarabia in 1812 after a war with Turkey which Napoleon had encouraged the Ottoman Empire to undertake in 1806, when France and Russia were fighting.

Napoleon was directly responsible for changes in the map of Scandinavia. Carrying out the provisions of Tilsit, Russia went to war with Sweden in 1808; by the Treaty of Friedrichshamm in 1809 it obtained Finland, with the agreement that the Finns would be permitted to retain their former institutions and would be bound to Russia only by the personal tie of having the same ruler (the tsar of Russia would be the grand duke of Finland).

When war between Russia and France was imminent, both sought the alliance of Sweden for the campaign of 1812. Napoleon promised Sweden, now administered by his former marshal, Jean Bernadotte, as crown prince, that it could regain Finland if it sided with him. Alexander countered with an offer at Denmark's expense: if Sweden became allied with Russia, it could annex Norway, which the British fleet had already cut off from Denmark. Sweden accepted the Russian bid, with the result that Finland remained part of the Russian Empire until the Revolution of 1917 and Norway remained a part of Sweden until 1905.

It was not only Europe whose map Napoleon affected. Overseas, too, the Napoleonic period was of decisive importance. Great Britain, exploiting its naval superiority, annexed several colonies. It also vastly extended its holdings in India while the other countries were preoccupied with Europe. Most of the gains in India were made by Marquess Richard Wellesley, governor-general of India from 1798 to 1805 and an older brother of the later Duke of Wellington. Among the areas over which he established control were Mysore, Tanjore, Surat, and the Carnatic.

THE NAPOLEONIC REVOLUTION

The Treaty of San Ildefonso of October 1, 1800, provided that Spain would return Louisiana to France. In 1802, availing himself of the chance afforded by Amiens to send an expeditionary force, Napoleon tried to put down a revolt in Santo Domingo led by Toussaint L'Ouverture. (There are some who say that he deliberately sent to the Caribbean the most republican elements in the army.) When the French were defeated by a combination of yellow fever and rebels, Napoleon decided that he could no longer hold on to his American possessions. Aware that the Americans could easily move in, he offered to sell Louisiana to the United States. But he was motivated in large part by his hostility to England; he did not want to run the risk that Louisiana might fall into the hands of his worst enemy:

> I renounce Louisiana. . . . This accession of territory confirms forever the power of the United States, and I have just given England a maritime rival that sooner or later will lay low her pride. . . . The English aspire to the disposition of all the riches in the world. I will be useful to the whole world if I am able to prevent their dominating America as they now dominate Asia.[16]

President Jefferson leaped at the opportunity to double the extent of his country by adding the territory between the Mississippi River and the Rocky Mountains, for 80 million francs ($16 million), and in 1803 the Louisiana Purchase became a reality.

Further changes in the overseas map resulted from a change of dynasty in Spain. In his attempt to enforce the Continental System, Napoleon felt that he could not trust the throne of Spain to the ruling Bourbons. He therefore effected the abdication of Charles IV and a renunciation of the throne by Charles' son Ferdinand, and declared his own brother Joseph the new Spanish king. These actions gave the colonists in Spanish America a pretext they had long been seeking. Desirous of running their affairs themselves rather than having officials from Spain im-

---

[16] Quoted in Elijah W. Lyon, *Louisiana in French Diplomacy, 1759–1804*. University of Chicago thesis, 1932, pp. 206–07.

posed on them, and anxious to trade with other countries free of mercantilistic restrictions imposed from the mother country, they now declared that their only allegiance was to the Bourbon ruling family. To Joseph Bonaparte they felt no sense of loyalty, and therefore declared themselves independent. Every Spanish-American colony had the start of an independence movement at this time. The fate of Spanish America was still uncertain in 1815, but it was obvious that Spain would not be able to restore in full its old colonial regime. Although it took some of the colonies until about 1825 to achieve independent status, the Napoleonic period had given them the opportunity to start marching up the freedom road.

When he moved into the Iberian Peninsula, Napoleon declared the House of Braganza deposed from the throne of Portugal. Taking its cue, the royal family fled to the colony of Brazil, frightened by only 6,000 French troops in all of Portugal and 1,500 in Lisbon. Never again subject to Portugal, Brazil became independent in 1822.

It is no wonder that some historians feel Napoleon's impact overseas was even greater than in Europe.

·IV·

THE LAWGIVER

France had received its first written constitutions during the time of the Revolution, and when Bonaparte and his confreres—products of the Revolution—seized power, they announced their intention of continuing constitutional government. In fact, Bonaparte in his speech to the Council of Elders during the *coup d'état* justified what the conspirators were doing by accusing Council members of violating the constitution.

On 20 Brumaire of Year VIII (November 11, 1799), the day after the completion of the coup, and on the demand of Bonaparte, twelve men were chosen to draft a constitution. Seven of them represented the Council of Five Hundred, five the Council of Elders. The select dozen included Lucien, Napoleon, and Abbé Sieyès, but Lucien played little part in the actual drafting.

The writers of the new fundamental law took into account the difficulties that had arisen during the Directory because neither the executive nor the legislative branch was supreme. The Directory itself, in the new constitutions it had prepared for the satellite republics, had tried to provide for a stronger executive branch. The drafting committee was determined to make the executive power stronger than the legislative.

Sieyès and Bonaparte agreed on this matter, but their concepts of the executive power did not coincide. Sieyès wanted to split the power between two consuls and to have a third for purely ceremonial purposes. Bonaparte, who wanted an all-powerful executive officer on the model of a general in the army, prevailed. (According to a story of the time, a Parisian who could not hear what was being said when the constitution was proclaimed in the streets asked what was in the constitution. "There is Bonaparte," was the reply.)

The Constitution of the Year VIII was a part of the Napoleonic revolution, and it made possible additional aspects of that revolution. Holders of land which had once belonged to the national government received a constitutional guarantee that they would not be dispossessed. Yet the Constitution was in some respects pre-Revolutionary or anti-Revolutionary. It contained no declaration of rights; the only right guaranteed was the inviolability of the home.

In considering whether the Constitution as a whole was in the Revolutionary tradition, we have to decide whether we mean the tradition of 1789, or of 1793—the time of the Terror—or of 1795, the period of moderate reaction. In 1789 the French, believing in the sovereignty of the people, wanted a type of government which would express that sovereignty and Rousseau's idea of the "general will." The best means of expressing popular sovereignty is by a one-house legislature; the more houses in a legislature, the easier to block effective action by it. The Constitution of 1791 had established a unicameral body, the Legislative Assembly, elected by holders of property on which at least a stated minimum direct tax was paid. The Constitution did not provide a parliamentary regime: the King appointed and dismissed the ministers, whose sole accountability was a judicial one for offenses against the Constitution or national security, attacks on property or liberty, and dissipation of departmental funds. The never-applied Constitution of the Year I (1793) pro-

CENTRAL   GOVERNMEN

FIRST CONSUL

SECOND CONSUL

THIRD CONSUL

The Ministers
Chosen by
and re-
sponsible to
the First
Consul

LOCAL   GOVERNMEN

PREFECTS*
Administrative heads
of departments

SUBPREFECTS**
Administrative heads
of arrondissements,
responsible to prefects

MAYORS**
(of communes
over 5,000)

MAYORS***
(of communes
under 5,000)

*Chosen by the First Consul from the Departmental List
**Chosen by the First Consul from the Communal List
***Chosen by the prefects from the Communal List

THE CONSTITUTION OF THE YEAR VIII

THE COUNCIL OF STATE

(drafts bills) 40 members chosen by the First Consul from the National List

THE TRIBUNATE

(discusses bills) 100 members chosen by the Senate from the National List

THE LEGISLATIVE BODY

(votes on bills) 300 members chosen by the Senate from the National List

THE SENATE

(decides constitutionality of bills) 60 members initially, 31 chosen by the Second and Third Consuls,* 29 by co-option; 2 added per year to bring total to 80. All chosen from the National List

ELECTORAL   PROCESS

THE NATIONAL LIST
(1/10 of the Departmental List)

THE DEPARTMENTAL LIST
(1/10 of the Communal List)

THE COMMUNAL LIST
(1/10 of all adult males)

*and by the Abbé Sieyès and Roger Ducos

ALL ADULT MALES

vided that all men could vote and hold office. That of the Year III reverted to the concept of rule by the propertied, but with a two-house rather than a unicameral legislature. Bonaparte's constitution was designed to put effective control in the hands of relatively few.

Bonaparte had no intention of creating a one-house legislature which would presumably have the final voice. Instead, following the ideas of Abbé Sieyès, his Constitution of the Year VIII created a three-house legislature; such a setup would make independent action by the legislature extremely difficult.

Bills were to be drawn up and proposed by a Council of State, which, it was later decided, would be composed of forty members appointed by the First Consul. Although the Council was engaged in the legislative process, the Constitution treated it as a part of the executive branch. Bills drafted by it were discussed by a Tribunate (note the classical terminology again) of a hundred members which decided in favor of or against the proposed legislation. The view of the Tribunate was not, however, binding; its activity really amounted to discussing without voting. Next, a *Corps législatif* (Legislative Body) voted without discussing. It listened to three members of the Tribunate, who presented the views of that body, and up to three members of the Council of State presenting the views of the government; then it cast its ballot. The sessions of both the Tribunate and the Legislative Body were open to the public, but in order to prevent such stampeding of the members as had taken place in Revolutionary assemblies, no more than two hundred spectators could attend at any one time. Topping the legislative sequence was a Conservative Senate, whose task was to "conserve" the Constitution by considering the constitutionality of any legislative enactment referred to it by the Tribunate or the Consuls.

The method of selecting the various legislative bodies, while giving lip service to the idea of popular sovereignty, effectively nullified it because of a system of co-optation. Ostensibly there was universal manhood suffrage, but this merely entitled each male to vote in a cantonal assembly for a "communal list" composed of one tenth of the number of voters.[1] Officials on the local level, up to and including the *arrondissement*,[2] would be selected by the authorities—not elected by the people—from this list. The communal list, in turn, selected a departmental list of one tenth of its number, and the departmental list chose one tenth of its members for a national list. Thus, only one man in a thousand had a theoretical chance to be named an official of the national government or a member of one of the national legislative bodies. From the national list the Senate chose the tribunes and legislators. In the Year VIII it enjoyed complete freedom of choice as no list of eligible notables had been drawn up in advance. One fifth of the membership of the Tribunate and the Legislative Body was to be renewed each year. Each department had at least one deputy in the Legislative Body, whose members had to be at least thirty years old.

At the time of its formation, the Senate was to have sixty members. Of this number, two were the ex-Directors and ex-conspirators, Sieyès and Roger Ducos. These two men and the Second and Third Consuls chose a majority of the Senate, which then selected the remainder. The number of senators, who served for life, was to increase by co-optation to eighty at the rate of two a year.

Superficially, Bonaparte went beyond the early Revolution in his application of popular sovereignty. He submitted the Constitution of the Year VIII to a plebiscite, a popular vote to see whether the people wanted the basic change in government that

[1] The distinguishing feature of a canton is that it is always the jurisdiction of a justice of the peace. The canton is a subdivision of an *arrondissement* and is the unit on which elections to the *arrondissement* council are based. Although the Directory had assigned it administrative tasks, Napoleon returned it to its normal function as an elective and judicial unit and reduced the number of cantons.

[2] The *arrondissement* was, and is, the largest subdivision of a department.

the Constitution entailed. (This had not been done for the Constitution of 1791, though it had been for the Constitutions of the Years I and III and for the annexation of such areas as Avignon and Venaissin in 1791.) An overwhelming majority, 3.5 million to about 1,500, voted in favor of the Constitution; but half of the eligible voters abstained from voting at all. But the Constitution was promulgated two months before the plebiscite and before any of the plebiscite machinery was even set in motion. The plebiscite also differed from earlier ones in that the voting registers remained open more than a month, during which time the government exerted all possible pressure for a favorable vote.

The Constitution of the Year VIII established a dictatorship. But Bonaparte, unsatisfied, moved toward more complete despotism.

The Tribunate as early as Year IX felt the oppressive and restrictive trend. The government claimed a right which severely reduced the influence of the Tribunate, that of deciding when the three tribunes would present the case of their colleagues to the Legislative Body. Even though the Tribunate did not exercise its constitutional right to advise the government on abuses to be corrected and improvements to be made, Bonaparte was annoyed by the opposition it furnished to such schemes of his as the establishment of special courts and the restriction of trial by jury. When the time came to replace a fifth of the members for the first time, in the Year X, Bonaparte asked the Senate to draw up a list of those who would remain. This he could do because the Constitution did not prescribe how to designate the fifth who would retire. Thus Bonaparte eliminated, legally, his most vocal critics. The Tribunate was divided into three sections, with every matter henceforth being considered by the appropriate section. Plenary sessions (of the whole body) met only to discuss treaties of peace or commerce; after 1804 the Tribunate could not hold such sessions at all. It was reduced to fifty members, renewed by half every three years; *arrondissement* colleges made the nominations, the Senate did the final selecting. In 1807 a *senatus consultum* (decree of the Senate) suppressed the Tribunate as a useless agency.

Although Bonaparte had nothing to fear from the Senate, in the Year X he established "senatorships," each of which was endowed with land and a manorial house. Up to one third of the senators could receive such benefices; Bonaparte chose the recipient of each such domain from a list of nominees drawn up by the Senate. Provision of this additional source of income effectively removed any trace of senatorial opposition. At the same time certain individuals became senators ex officio, and Bonaparte received the right to name additional members up to a total of 120. When he became Emperor, the limitation on the number of senators he could appoint was removed.

Napoleon used the Senate to accomplish various ends. In 1801 it deported 130 Jacobins without trial on charges of an attempt on Bonaparte's life, and in the next year it prescribed the methods of renewal for the Tribunate and Legislative Body. Napoleon also used the Senate, in a way unforeseen by the Constitution of the Year VIII, to legislate without consulting the other legislative bodies, and even to revise the Constitution in his favor, by issuing *senatus consulta*. Such actions were excused by citing the Senate's task of conserving the Constitution.

The first constitutional revision took place in the Year X (1802), when the Senate's amendments, almost as long as the original document, in effect supplanted the Constitution of the Year VIII. The most important provision was that Bonaparte should now be Consul for life. The method of voting in the plebiscite was the same as two years earlier; this time there were five times as many opposed, most of whom came from the right rather than the left. This constitution lessened the powers of the legislative bodies and extended those of the First Consul. He now got the right to convoke the Senate, and to convoke and dismiss the Legislative Body, whose president he named. He also named the presidents of the cantonal assemblies and the electoral colleges. He could negotiate treaties of alliance and peace without the preliminary approval of the legislature.

At this time it was provided that members of the departmental electoral colleges should be chosen from among the 600 largest taxpayers. In addition to the members elected for life, the colleges also had up to twenty members chosen by Bonaparte from the thirty most heavily taxed people in the department. These electoral colleges, departmental and communal, were an innovation which lasted until 1848. They meant an electoral aristocracy based on wealth.

Another development that had lasting impact was the establishment of the empire. This was effected by the Constitution of the Year XII, a *senatus consultum* of May 18, 1804. The question put to plebiscite vote this time was: "The people wishes the hereditary transmission of the imperial dignity in the direct, natural, legitimate, and adoptive descendance of Napoleon Bonaparte and in the direct, natural, and legitimate descendance of Joseph Bonaparte and Louis Bonaparte." The matter of whether Napoleon should be Emperor was taken for granted and never came into popular question. Napoleon as Emperor did have to swear to uphold "equality of rights, political and civil liberty, and the irrevocability of sales of national property." Even earlier there had been the beginnings of a court; assumption of the title of "Emperor" led to an imperial nobility.

Napoleon was responsible for one more constitution in France, the Additional Act to the Constitutions of the Empire, during the Hundred Days in 1815. This document was the handiwork of Benjamin Constant, at one time an implacable foe of Bonaparte in the Tribunate. Constant was a leading liberal, and the document he wrote and which received Napoleon's approbation, though it never went into effect, was liberal—Napoleon had to be at least as liberal as Louis XVIII, whom he was overthrowing.

The Additional Act provided for a constitutional monarchy with a ministry which the legislature could call to account, freedom of religion, and a free press, and it broadened the basis of suffrage. The major importance of the Additional Act was that it served that part of the Napoleonic legend which portrayed Napoleon as a liberal who had been forced by circumstances to postpone putting his desires into execution.

Napoleon also gave constitutions to several of his vassal states. Among them were the kingdoms of Italy, Naples, Holland, Spain, and Westphalia; the grand duchies of Berg, Frankfurt, and Würzburg; and the Illyrian Provinces. But the practice did not always coincide with the statute books. Murat never applied the constitution in Naples, and in Spain Joseph was able to do so only in part. Only in Holland did the legislature function, and in each of the states ruled by a relative of Napoleon the king's power tended to increase. One of the most important of the constitutions was that which Bavaria got in 1808; with it Bavaria passed from a patrimony of the prince to a state with public law. Baden's constitution brought significant strides toward centralization, as did that of Württemberg.

The Constitution of the Year VIII, by its very vagueness as to how administrative officials should be chosen, enabled the despotically inclined Bonaparte to effect a centralization of the government. The Bourbon rulers of France had sought this ever since the time of Henry IV at the start of the 17th century, though Louis XVI had betrayed the centralizing process in the years immediately preceding the Revolution. The early Revolutionaries were so interested in freedom, especially freedom from despotism and arbitrary tyranny, that they abandoned the search. The localities now had so much autonomy that government tended to fall apart, and the situation brought about a Reign of Terror. With the Terror France once again set out on the path of centralization; the National Convention was theoretically in charge, but its committees were actually at the controlling point. The committees worked through revolutionary clubs and societies, especially those associated with the Jacobin Club of Paris. Following the Terror, federalism rather than centralization became the watchword. Under Bonaparte the centralization was achieved; he was able to effect it rapidly because the Revolution had prepared the way and the vast majority of Frenchmen were willing to accept it: the earlier decentralization had put France in the deadly peril from enemies within and without that had made the Terror seem necessary.

Despite their striving for centralization of authority, the Bourbons had never been able to obtain uniformity in the administrative structure of France. This the Revolutionaries did achieve.[3] At first they created eighty-three departments; the number was increased as new lands were annexed. When Bonaparte came to power, there were ninety-eight. If the Revolution had not cleared away the earlier chaos, Napoleon could not have achieved his administrative uniformity.

Bonaparte retained the general outlines of the Revolutionary administrative organization. The Constitution of the Year III had eliminated the district as an administrative unit; Bonaparte restored it in the form of a communal *arrondissement* headed by a subprefect. In 1800 there were 420 such units, four or five per department. The competence of the *arrondissements* was extremely limited; they did not even have budgets. The smallest administrative unit was the commune.

Napoleon did effect one basic change: as First Consul and as Emperor he appointed a wide variety of administrative officials—prefects and subprefects and their councils, police commissioners, and mayors and their deputies in towns with more than 5,000 inhabitants. The mayors of smaller towns were appointed by the prefect of the department, who was in charge of all municipal action. In 1800 there were 30,000 mayors, and the number in-

---

[3] See Chapter I for a discussion of government during the *ancien régime* and of how the National Assembly changed it.

creased as France annexed territory. The unprecedented degree of personal centralized control Napoleon obtained through this appointive procedure led one of his biographers to write, "The day of the powerful unified state had arrived."

The Constitution of the Year VIII created a corps of French functionaries. Prior to then the term "functionary" had applied to a representative of the people as well as to a government agent, but after that date only to the latter. Napoleon found himself handicapped, however, by a lack of capable officials. To train administrators knowing both theory and practice, he re-created the positions of auditor in 1803 and of master of requests in 1806.[4] Auditors, the less important and more numerous of the two positions, aided the Council of State, ministers in charge of executive departments, judges, and provincial councils. Masters of requests functioned primarily as legal advisers to the Council of State. The two types of posts are still a part of the French governmental system.

The details of local administration appeared not in the Constitution, but in a law of 28 Pluviôse, Year VIII (February 17, 1800). The centralization it achieved was discerned by the *Publiciste* in its issue of February 19:

From the First Consul to the mayor of a village in the Pyrenees, everything holds together, all the links of the great chain are tightly bound together. The movement of power will be rapid as it will traverse a line whose points it surpasses. It will find everywhere execution and nowhere opposition, always instruments and no obstacles against it.[5]

The essential person in this administrative chain was the prefect in the department; as the French historian Alexis de Tocqueville pointed out, he was a reincarnation of the intendant of the

---

[4] Both types of officials, though with different functions, had existed during the *ancien régime*.

[5] Quoted in J.-J. Chevallier, *Histoire des institutions politiques de la France moderne (1789–1945)*. Paris: Dalloz, 1958, p. 133.

old regime. The prefect alone was charged with administration. He was aided by a council of prefecture to handle administrative claims, and a general council, which sat only two weeks a year to allocate taxes. The latter's financial competence constituted the only restriction on the prefect's sphere of authority. Such a centralized system was of course contradictory to the system of elective self-government introduced by the Revolution. The constitutions which Holland and Naples later received indicate that Napoleon intended to eliminate the elective principle. In Naples all the members of the unicameral legislature were to be appointed by the king. Louis in Holland could appoint all new legislators as others rotated out of office.

In municipal administrations as well as elsewhere the regime of franchise based on property was continued. The Constitution of the Year X stipulated that candidates for seats on a municipal council had to be among the hundred most highly taxed citizens of the canton. The centralization likewise increased when the Consulate for Life was established, for the new constitution permitted Bonaparte to choose a municipal tax collector from among three men nominated by the municipal council. Each commune of more than 5,000 had a police commissioner. Paris had a second prefect, a prefect of police, subordinate to the national Minister of Police (except for the years 1802–04 when the Ministry of Police was eliminated) for strictly police functions, and to the Minister of the Interior for all other functions.

One of the most important institutions Bonaparte continued from the Directory was the Secretariat of State, which he transformed into a Ministry of State under Hugues Maret. Since the ministry handled all documents passing between Napoleon and the executive departments, Napoleon was able to supervise the departments without giving them any collective responsibility.

To the end of his reign Napoleon continued this administrative reorganization, appointing more and more officials as time went on. In the Year X he created the Privy Council, initially to prepare *senatus consulta*. Another important type of body he established was the "Councils of Administration," which played a role virtually as important as that of the Council of State. Sitting on the councils were interested ministers, their chiefs of service, some councillors of state, and sometimes even provincial officials.

Under Napoleon the police system was greatly extended; his government, in fact, became the forerunner of the modern police state. The Ministry of General Police, utilizing an effective secret police force, subdued all political opposition. Napoleon daily received a police bulletin giving him information on a wide variety of items: public opinion, the press, the clergy, desertions, and so on.

What was the lasting importance of Napoleon's administrative innovations? He developed a system of government that became a model for later dictatorships. Bonaparte reverted to the *ancien régime* to get the desired centralization, a centralization that enabled him to get things done and furnished him the desired men, money, and order; but the idea of specialists working together under a co-ordinating head was novel in his day. The government was an oligarchy of officials and experts all subject to one man's disposition. Napoleon made the administrative framework decisive. He had in mind the use of administration to unify France and the French. "With a good administration all individuals will forget the factions of which they have been made members and they will be permitted to be French."

The spirit of the Year VIII still pervades France's administration. With some modifications Napoleon's administrative framework has lasted through numerous changes of political constitution, functioning even when the personnel was mediocre. Though mayors are now elected, the prefects are still chosen by the central government, under the present Fifth Republic by the Council of Ministers.

But the story goes beyond France. The administrative system spread to other regions, in some of which it has lasted to the present day. The administrative system of Italy, for example, is firmly rooted in that of Napoleon; that of Holland until 1848 came from the French occupation.

One field that the Constitution of the Year VIII tended to slight was the judiciary. The Constitution outlined the different kinds of courts, but said nothing about their number except that each communal *arrondissement* was to have at least one justice of the peace, elected for a period of three years, and that there would be one Court of Cassation for all France. The judges of this court, the highest court in France, were to be chosen by the Senate from the list of national notables. But the courts were not to interpret the laws; initially this was done by the Council of State, in 1806 Napoleon assumed the prerogative himself. The Constitution retained from the Revolution such practices as the use of grand and trial juries, arbitration, and the handling of conciliation by justices of the peace.

Bonaparte shortly had to turn his attention to putting flesh on the judicial skeleton provided for in the Constitution. To a large extent he merely re-established the system created by the Revolution; there has been no substantial change in the French judicial structure since his time. In 1802 the judicial hierarchy was re-established, with each level having supervision (including powers of censure and discipline) over the one below it. Thus, the Court of Cassation supervised the criminal courts and the courts of appeal, and the latter supervised the civil courts, which looked after the justices of the peace. Such a hierarchical organization was of course centralization in another sphere. After the Year X justices of the peace were appointed by Bonaparte from two names submitted by the cantonal assembly. Other judges Bonaparte chose from the list of departmental notables.

The Constitution provided that judges would serve for life unless they were removed from the list of eligibles. In the Year X irremovability seemingly became absolute with the elimination of the lists of notables. But in 1807 life tenure was reserved until after a judge had sat five years. Napoleon used this new provision to purge the ranks of the judges. The number of judges increased because of the creation of 400 *arrondissement* and 28 appellate courts, one for every three departments. In 1801 special criminal courts were created to deal with the Chouans, the royalist guerrillas in the West of France. These courts functioned not only there, but in a total of thirty-two departments.

Justice tended to become arbitrary. The creation of numerous exceptional courts was a step in this direction; for example, temporary Courts of Assizes replaced the criminal courts in 1810 for reasons of economy. Bonaparte did not favor the jury system; his attitude was revealed in a provision that the Senate could quash the verdict of a jury as being prejudicial to the state. Justice tended to become class justice because of the qualifications required for jury duty. A juror had to belong to one of several categories of people, any one of which would set him apart from the average Frenchman. He might be a member of an electoral college; one of the most highly taxed individuals in the country; a person paying a high rent; an official chosen by Napoleon; a member of a learned society; or a person with a doctor's degree.

A decree of March 1810 authorized the Privy Council to make punitive arrests. Theoretically these were for a maximum of a year; the reality was quite different. An order signed by the Minister of Police and the grand judge also sufficed to put a man in jail; again there was a theoretical limit, of ten days, but no authority seemed concerned about it.

France desperately needed for its laws a uniformity such as the Revolution and the Consulate had given its administration. Southern France was guided by Roman law. Northern France was guided by customary, or common, law. In addition, there were 366 local codes of law, so that a learned legist in one part of the country might be considered a legal illiterate in another part.

Unity of laws had been demanded in most of the *cahiers* of 1789, the statements of grievances drawn up by the voters of the electoral units. A uniform system of law would have been in keeping with the enlightenment of the century. The Constitution of 1791 adopted by the National Assembly stated, "A code of civil laws common to the whole kingdom will be drawn up." The Revolutionaries saw the danger to their idea of unity in the multitudinous codes of law and had tried on two different occasions to devise a single code, but without success. The leader of the second attempt was Jean Cambacérès, whom Bonaparte later, during the Consulate, selected as a member of the commission to draft a new code of civil law for France.

Napoleon on St. Helena, in the exile of the last years of his life, is reported to have said, "My glory is not to have won forty battles, for Waterloo's defeat will destroy the memory of as many victories. But what nothing will destroy, what will live eternally, is my Civil Code." Historians agree that this is his main claim to fame; a recent biographer calls it one of the few documents which have influenced the whole world.

The Revolution had made such a codification possible by doing away with feudal law, eliminating local interests which blocked unification of the law, and strengthening a united national consciousness; Bonaparte served as the catalyst to bring to completion something long desired. He chose the first propitious occasion to codify the law. Such a codification could not have been achieved earlier because it was necessary first for the great reforms of the Revolution to be carried out and for the country to accept the new regime. Bonaparte appointed the commission, which included some distinguished jurists from both the south and the north of France. He prodded it into action when it lagged. The "Commission of Legislation" of the Council of State devoted 102 sessions to discussing the proposed code; Bonaparte presided over 57 of them. He intervened in the discussion frequently and effectively (more often to deal with the rights of women than for any other topic).

Bonaparte wanted to restate the law in one complete package, letting experience dictate the final choice when there was a conflict between Revolutionary and pre-Revolutionary laws. The Code was further inspired by the idea of remaking the law in the image of a new and better society, of clarifying and hence to a degree reforming the law in terms of natural law. This was consonant with the ideas of the 18th century, which desired unity, clarity, and simplicity.

The individual parts of the Code went into effect as they were adopted; on March 21, 1804, the articles of these thirty-six laws were united into a Civil Code, one of the most notable events in all legal history. In its final form the Code was noted for a clarity and conciseness of style that led the French novelist Stendhal to say he read it every day to capture its qualities. These features contributed greatly to its success, for the French could easily understand it. In 1807 the Code received the name Code Napoléon, a name richly deserved.

Did the Code Napoléon continue or reverse the Revolutionary tradition? The Legislative Body turned down the one title submitted to it, and the Tribunate turned down two, on the grounds that the Code was not sufficiently Revolutionary and that the draft had been made too hastily.[6] After the rejection, Bonaparte withdrew all the titles from consideration until after the purge of the Year X discussed above; these actions of the Tribunate and Legislative Body on the Code were a powerful reason for Bonaparte's method of renewal of the two bodies at that time.

The Code was a moderate document designed to reconcile opposing groups in the population; it therefore inevitably had to discard part of the Revolutionary and part of the traditional thinking. For example, it reversed the Revolutionary ban on wills, but it placed limits on how men could dispose of their real property. There were compromises between authority and individualism, freedom of will and public interest, protection of

[6] The Code is divided into books, titles, chapters, sections, and articles. A "title" is thus a relatively large subdivision of the entire work.

property and individual wealth. Even those parts, such as bourgeois protection of property, which some of the French looked on as reactionary—and these were due not to Bonaparte, but to the lawyers—were progressive or even revolutionary for the rest of Europe.

In most respects the Code continued the Revolutionary tradition and accepted the social principles of 1789. It retained the basic principles underlying Revolutionary law—equality of all in the eyes of the law, freedom of conscience, secularity of the state, and freedom of work. The Revolutionists, men of the 18th-century enlightenment, believed in economic freedom; the prohibition on associations proclaimed in the Le Chapelier law of 1791 was repeated in the Code. By stating that "contracts legally formed take the place of law for those who have made them," the Code reinforced economic liberalism and contributed to the growth of capitalism.

The Code compromised between the ideas of the *ancien régime* and the Revolution on the matter of the family, which the drafters treated as the basic institution of civilized society. The family was the one institution standing between the individual and the nation which the Code fostered. Care was taken, however, that the family should not become too strong; for example, the right to make wills was limited so that succession and inheritance would not create a new hereditary aristocracy. The Code restated the idea that the head of the family was the real authority, and even permitted him to put his children in jail—one month for those under sixteen, six months for those sixteen and over to age twenty-one—without requiring the approval of any governmental authority. The Code took an anti-Revolutionary step, though it did not go all the way back to the *ancien régime,* in subjecting the marriage rights of sons and daughters to varying degrees of parental control, depending on age and sex.

During the *ancien régime,* matters pertaining to marriage—which was considered a sacrament—were subject to the jurisdiction of the church courts; the Revolution had secularized all such matters, while abolishing the church courts, and the Code retained this secularization. The civil marriage had to be performed before a religious marriage took place. The Revolution had permitted divorce; Bonaparte was very interested in seeing the Code retain this, but in more restricted fashion than under the Revolution, and, as will be seen below, not on equal terms for men and women. Only three grounds for divorce were recognized: adultery, conviction of a serious crime, and grave insults, excesses, or cruelty. Incompatibility, which had been given as the reason for the vast majority of divorces, no longer sufficed. Bonaparte insisted on inserting divorce by mutual agreement, designed to keep private an actual ground for divorce. If the couple had been married at least two years but no longer than twenty they might legally separate. The restored Bourbons eliminated the right of divorce in 1816, and it was not again legalized until 1884 under the Third Republic.

In large part the family was considered from the viewpoint of property and inheritance. The Code did not go so far as the Revolution, which had provided for equal distribution among his heirs of the property of a deceased person, for it permitted persons to draw up wills disposing freely of one fourth of their property. This was not enough to enable the testator to effect any important inequality among his children. Bonaparte clearly differentiated between legitimate and illegitimate children; the latter he cut off from any inheritance, stating, "Society has no interest in having these bastards recognized." Adoption was retained, in accordance with Revolutionary legislation.

The Code regressed from the Revolution in assigning to women a decidedly inferior status. An unmarried woman could not be part of the family council, serve as a guardian, or witness a legal document. The husband received almost complete control over community property. A wife owed obedience to her husband, and she needed special authorization for each civil act. Thus the Code extended to all France disabilities previously known only in the Roman law provinces. Inequality in the male-female relationship was particularly shocking in the matter of divorce. A husband might demand divorce for adultery if the wife tried to introduce a stranger into the legitimate family; she could obtain a divorce only if the husband cohabited with his concubine in the common house. The husband could have his wife shut up in a house of correction for up to two years, but a fine was the severest penalty a wife's charges could bring upon her husband. If the husband murdered his wife upon surprising her in adultery, his act was legally justifiable; if the circumstances were reversed the murder she committed was inexcusable.[7]

The Code made irrevocable the disappearance of the feudal aristocracy which the Revolution had accomplished. This was, in fact, one of the main preoccupations of the drafters of the Code. It meant that wherever the Code went, feudal institutions and rights vanished, and herein the Code crystallized and organized the spirit of the Revolution. Where such restrictions existed, the Code also effected the elimination of rule by the clergy through secularization of the state, and of social castes by opening all occupations to all men. In most cases, former serfs had to indemnify their landlords.

Of the 2,281 articles of the Code, the vast majority pertain to property. Landed property particularly interested Bonaparte; his Code, which was designed primarily for an agricultural economy, paid little attention to personal property. But it was aimed at satisfying holders of real property, and was thus a middle-class

[7] In the spring of 1965 the government of President Charles de Gaulle introduced into the National Assembly a bill which has been designated a new bill of women's rights. When it became law on July 13, 1965—with very little publicity—it amended the Code Napoléon to give married women a status equal to their husbands'. Husband and wife are now partners who own their personal possessions and manage joint property on an equal footing. Furthermore, penalties for adultery are now the same for the man and for the wife.

document. The Code made no provision for entail, thus facilitating purchase of property from former nobles by members of the middle class. By continuing the Revolutionary ban on primogeniture, it enabled all sons in a family to obtain an inheritance —an inheritance which tended to give them a bourgeois outlook on life. The provisions on inheritance made France through much of the 19th century a nation of small farmer-owners. Ownership was defined in a far more modern way than had existed before the Revolution: "The right of enjoying and disposing of things in the most absolute manner." It was now a complete, absolute, free, and simple right.

In keeping with the spirit of '89, the wage-earner was left subject to the ups and downs of economic competition. The Code's continuation of the 1791 prohibition on workingmen's organizations placed the laborer at the mercy of his employer. In disputes between a worker and his employer, the word of the latter was to be accepted. All that the Code did for non-owners was to protect their personal freedom by forbidding them to lease property or hire out their services for an indefinite period.

In addition to the Civil Code, five other codes were drawn up. The Rural Code was never adopted; those which went into effect were a Code of Civil Procedure in 1806, a Commercial Code in 1807, a Code of Criminal Procedure in 1808, and a Penal Code in 1810. The Penal Code was both progressive and reactionary: reactionary in that it provided for severe and unjust penalties— among them branding, and the cutting off of a hand for parricide in addition to decapitation; progressive in its provision for minimum and maximum rather than fixed penalties. The Code of Criminal Procedure was reactionary in that it permitted arbitrary arrest and partially re-established the secrecy of court proceedings that had prevailed during the *ancien régime;* the accused could no longer hear the testimony against him.

Each of the codes was adopted in some non-French areas, but

the real success story is that of the Code Napoléon. In his *History of Europe,* H. A. L. Fisher comments:

> More than any other influence the Civil Code spread through Europe the fame of the institutions of the new France. Here was the pith and kernel of the revolutionary philosophy in a shape made practical for the use of men. Here was a combination of fruitful innovation and ancient usage. Here was liberty combined with order. Not since the Institutes of Justinian has any compendium of law been so widely copied.[8]

Albert Sorel, a well-known and judicious historian of the French Revolution period, wrote:

> The *Code Civil* has remained, for the peoples [of the world], the French Revolution—organized. When one speaks of the benefits of this Revolution and of the liberating role of France, one thinks of the *Code Civil,* one thinks of this application of the idea of justice to the realities of life.

The entire Code, the book that made such a tremendous impact, was only about twice the length of this volume.

Although Napoleon's administrative system spread to some non-French areas, the expansion of the Code reached farther. Napoleon wanted it accepted as widely as possible. He looked upon the Code as a means of increasing the ruler's power in satellite states governed through his relatives, by eliminating feudalism and by making the priests less dangerous. He informed Joseph in Naples of this in so many words:

> The Code will confirm your power because it does away with everything that is not protected by entails and no great estates will remain except such fiefs as you will found. . . . This is what has made me preach the need of a civil code and has persuaded me to introduce it.

Napoleon further thought that the Code would strengthen the position of France. To Louis in Holland he wrote, "Having the same civil laws . . . tightens the bond of nations." When Louis

---

[8] *A History of Europe from the Beginning of the 18th Century to 1937.* London: Eyre and Spottiswood, 1952, p. 839.

showed himself reluctant to accept the Code, Napoleon castigated him: "I don't see why you need so much time or what changes must be made. . . . A nation of eighteen hundred thousand cannot have a separate Code. The Romans gave their laws to their allies—why should not France have hers adopted in Holland?" The Code was the essential part of Napoleon's social policy that gave him a chance to reconcile the *bourgeoisie* and peasants to his rule. His outlook on the Code was the classical one of the 18th century—there was only one standard, a universal one. He told Louis, "If you tamper with the Napoleonic Code, it will no longer be the Napoleonic Code." The concept of the Code as being based on universal principles of human reason served as one motive for introducing it into foreign territories.

Although he sometimes had to use pressure, Napoleon was able to get the Code put into effect in all satellite areas. Holland received the Code in unadulterated form after becoming part of the French Empire; Louis's refusal to adopt it in its entirety was one reason for his downfall as king of Holland. The Pope opposed the introduction of the Code into Italy because of its provision for divorce, and the Papal States were the last in the Italian peninsula to receive the Code.

Despite Napoleon's attitude in general that the Code should be adopted *in toto,* he sometimes permitted rulers in dependent states to effect modifications. In Warsaw the peasants were no longer attached to the land, but the land remained the lord's. Feudal rights, land dues, the *corvée,*[9] and the tithe all remained in effect. Equality before the law, however, lasted even after Napoleon's downfall. The wars and the need for humoring allied rulers prevented Napoleon, in the relatively short time at his disposal, from effecting reforms as deep-seated as he would have liked. The princes in the Confederation of the Rhine spared

[9] The seigniorial *corvée,* not the royal. Both were unpaid labor owed by the peasant. The royal *corvée* was solely on the roads; although there were three kinds of seigniorial *corvée,* it, too, was usually work on the roads.

the aristocracy; although they effected a profound transformation in the law of their realms in the half-dozen years after 1806, because they wanted to be ready for any combination of Napoleonic victories or defeats, the bond between the monarchy and the nobility remained unbroken in their states. Bavaria adopted only the Penal Code, and each of the regions in the kingdom kept its customary law. Despite keeping many of its prerogatives, the nobility was no longer so powerful as the monarchy. In Württemberg, feudal institutions and the old social regime were not suppressed, though personal servitude was abolished.

Some areas not controlled by Napoleon also adopted at least a modified version of the Code because they saw in it something good to be imitated. Louisiana in 1808 adopted a code of laws closely resembling the Napoleonic Code, and a second code of 1825 was even closer to that of Napoleon.[10] Latin America also felt the impact. The original Code is still in effect in the Dominican Republic, the Bolivian code is little more than a translation. The code of Chile, though more original, owes its arrangement and many passages to the Napoleonic Code. That of Uruguay is similar to the French Code, which also exerted a strong influence on Argentina's codification. Elsewhere in America the Quebec code adheres to the form of the Napoleonic Code.

In the first century and a half of its life the Napoleonic Code was introduced into thirty-five states and adapted in thirty-five more. Rumania in 1864 adopted a code which was a literal translation of the French Code. Likewise the Code served as the model for Egypt. Even Communist Yugoslavia, influenced by its own history and going back to the adoption of the Napoleonic Code in the Illyrian Provinces, now a part of its territory, has a legal system under the impress of the Code. In the Rhineland

---

[10] Although these statements about Louisiana are accurate, we should not overlook the strong impact of the Spanish legal code on that of Louisiana. There is a tendency to omit mention of this in history books.

the Code lasted until the end of the 19th century; in Luxemburg and Belgium it is still in effect. Japan adopted a similar code in 1898, after almost two decades of its application without official approval. Mauritius, though no longer a part of the French Empire, follows the Code literally; any change effected in metropolitan France is automatically adopted on the island.

Even in places such as Holland, Germany, Switzerland, Italy, and Illyria, where the Code did not outlive the Empire, it made a strong imprint on the civil laws of the region. Abolition of the Code brought such confusion and chaos in certain countries that they returned to it. In the Italian peninsula, for example, the Two Sicilies in 1812[11] and Parma, Modena, and Sardinia later adopted codes derived from the Code Napoléon. The code of the Kingdom of Italy, adopted in 1864, likewise had its source in the Napoleonic Code. The Belgians, who were incorporated in the Kingdom of the Netherlands from 1815 to 1830, fought so strongly for the Napoleonic Code that, even after they had broken away, Holland in 1838 adopted a code based on Napoleon's.

The Code Napoléon so impressed governments, even those which did not adopt it, that the 19th century became the great century of legal codification. In addition to the countries mentioned above, Austria, Portugal, Spain, Germany, and Turkey all adopted civil codes. But that of Napoleon easily predominates in the civil-law, as opposed to common-law, world.

One reason for the lasting success of the French Code is that, like the Constitution of the United States, it is a flexible instrument. It guided France through many changes of government and during the transition from an agricultural to a modern capitalistic country. It should be noted, however, that French courts have modified it, and that it has been revised since World War II. The Constitution of 1946, for example, granted women

---

[11] At this time, the kingdom included only the island of Sicily, as Murat ruled the Kingdom of Naples.

equal political and civil rights. But this grant worked only in theory and for single women.

The Code contributed greatly to Napoleon's achievement of helping France turn away from the past. It cemented the ideas of freedom of person and of contract (including the right to enter any occupation), equality of all Frenchmen, and freedom of civil society from ecclesiastical control. As the first truly modern code of laws, the Code Napoléon for the first time in modern history gave a nation a unified system of law applicable to all citizens without distinction.[12] By providing uniformity of laws it further promoted the national unity fostered by the Revolution. Its entire outlook gave a further impulse to the rise of the *bourgeoisie*. A threatened disintegration of the family under the Convention and Directory was sharply halted, and the family once again became the most important social institution. J. J. Chevallier says, in his book on French political institutions:

It is not a creation, but a co-ordination. It summed up the whole long historical tradition of the past, vivified and renewed by the Revolution, and it could be adapted to the society which issued from the crisis. . . . It safeguarded some of the essential privileges of the Revolution. Being national, it has been an agent of unity, it is *common* to all Frenchmen.[13]

The very act of codification, marking the end of a period of legal development, tended to make the Revolution firm and lasting.

[12] Great Britain, whose system was based on common rather than codified law, still had entail and the privileges of the House of Lords.

[13] *Op. cit.*, p. 163.

· V ·

THE FINANCIER AND ECONOMIST

Were Napoleon's financial and economic policies dictated solely by expediency, or were they partly inspired by the theories of the 18th century? Historians have long pondered this question without reaching a final answer. Here it suffices to note that his government's fiscal policy was, on the whole, one of the triumphs of Napoleon's career and an achievement that has had a lasting impact. Somewhat less successful in the economic field, he nonetheless attempted to stimulate the economy of France and the territories under its control and did bring about several innovations.

The inability of the Directory to solve its fiscal problems helped pave the way for the seizure of power by Bonaparte and his fellow conspirators. The Directory had discontinued paying interest on two thirds of the government debt; this naturally angered the government's creditors. The amount of paper money in circulation in the form of *assignats* (which had the confiscated land of the church as supposed security, except that the amount issued surpassed the value of the land by 1300 per cent) had grown unmanageable. The Directory had therefore replaced most of the assignats with a new form of paper money, known as territorial warrants, which soon sank on the exchange to one per cent of face value. The Directory next refused to accept these forms of paper money in payment of taxes. But other kinds of depreciated paper were still circulating when Bonaparte became consul.

Bonaparte realized that his government would not be able to remain in power, even though it might win military victories, if he did not restore some order to the finances. One of his first goals, therefore, was balancing the budget. This was not a simple task, but he succeeded in doing so for the Year IX, which began about ten and a half months after the start of the Consulate. He accomplished the feat largely by exacting contributions from conquered areas. In addition he whittled down expenses and collected taxes more energetically. His later budgets were rarely balanced, but the consolidated debt of France remained relatively small, particularly in comparison with that of England, and amounted to only 60 million francs in 1814. The debt was kept down, however, only by Napoleon's conquests and the resulting contributions that helped defray the expenses of the military, ranging from half to three fourths of the total budget.

Napoleon did not rely on tribute, but levied numerous new taxes—which led to one of his outstanding fiscal achievements, the creation of a solid financial administration. He began with direct taxes. Eight days after assuming power, he abolished the forced loan imposed by the Directory, and replaced it with a 25 per cent surtax on personal and property taxes.[1] A central agency was later established under a collector-general. In addition, each department had a general collector of taxes and each *arrondissement* a special collector. The most radical aspect of the new system was that the collectors had to make an advance deposit of

[1] A forced loan is merely a tax by what is, hopefully, a more agreeable name. That of the Directory was progressive, with the rich supposedly paying a higher percentage of their income than those less well-to-do. A surtax is a tax on taxes.

a certain proportion of the estimated tax yield; in practice this meant that only the rich could be tax collectors.

Fully aware that people do not like taxes—all the worker and peasant *cahiers* of 1789 had requested lighter and more fairly allocated taxes—Bonaparte tried to make payment as palatable as possible. His sugar-coating policy included substituting a larger proportion of indirect for direct taxes so that the average Frenchman would not know just how or how much he was paying. Among these taxes were excise and transaction taxes on beer, wine, and hard liquor. In 1804 the government created an administration of indirect taxes (*droits réunis*) to handle all such taxes as those on alcohol, playing cards, and tobacco. Thus it brought into being a new corps of functionaries, responsible to the Minister of Finance, Martin Gaudin, and also to the Chamber of Accounts. In 1806 Napoleon reinstituted a salt tax, to replace and bring in more revenue than the unpopular highway tax; consumption of salt promptly fell. The government also took over a monopoly on tobacco at the end of 1810; the Bourbon government had likewise had one, and such a monopoly has persisted to the present day.

The tax administration soon gave proof of its efficacy. Under Napoleon the French, who have long shown a penchant and a talent for not paying taxes, came closer to meeting their obligations than at any earlier time or most later times. He was able to collect between 430 and 500 million francs a year.

In an attempt to make sure that these obligations were equitable, Bonaparte in the Year X ordered the formation of a commission to determine how to allocate real-estate taxes with the greatest possible equality. The commission demanded a survey of ownership. Its recommendation was in keeping with the feeling of the Revolutionaries that only a cadaster, or general survey of the whole nation for appraisal purposes, could make sure everybody paid his fair share; the Convention had ordered a general cadaster in 1793, but, despite increasing evidence of the need

101

for one, it was begun only under the Consulate. A survey of the communes, treating each as a whole, made no attempt to uncover assessment discrepancies within an individual commune, where they were most apparent to the individual. Thus no basis existed for removing tax inequalities. A law of September 15, 1807, ordered a general survey of each parcel of land, such as the Convention had had in mind. Until the survey was completed in a commune, the value of a parcel of land was to be determined by acts of sale or by the amount charged for leases. The principle of stability of cadastral evaluations laid down by the 1807 law, that an assessment would remain fixed for a long time and would be changeable only with respect to gains or losses of taxable items, has governed French evaluation ever since. Although Napoleon devoted 55 million francs to the cadaster ordered in 1807, it was far from complete at the end of his reign. By that time a maximum of 6,000 communes out of a total of 44,000 had been surveyed. The cadaster did not lead to truly equitable results until 1821; then the law dealt with individuals in each commune rather than concerning itself with equity for all the communes in a canton.

Napoleon's contribution to taxation policy lay in asserting the principle that taxes should be fair and stable in practice as well as in theory, and in initiating a general and complete assessment of real property. The mere fact that such practice has become commonplace illustrates the importance of his tax program.

The rapidity with which paper currency of various types had sunk to low levels following the outbreak of war in 1792, and its continuance at those levels, may have persuaded Bonaparte to eliminate the bad paper from the market by a partial bankruptcy in 1800. This took the form of announcing that the government would not pay army contractors for the supplies it had bought on credit and that it would not honor certain types of bonds. Although specie was in short supply at the time, Bonaparte next declared that only specie would be legal tender. Despite frequent complaints about the lack of specie, its amount was increasing. So was its rate of circulation as hoarding declined. A law of 7 Germinal, Year XI (March 27, 1803), established the ratio between gold and silver at 15.5–1 and determined what size pieces would be coined. But silver rather than gold was the standard for the franc, at five grains per franc. This law fixed the money charter of France for 125 years. Bonaparte completed this series of currency measures by offering to coin, without cost, the bullion that citizens brought to the government mint. For the first time France had a clearly defined currency whose real and face values coincided.

Creation of a sound currency made possible the completion of the next basic project of Napoleon's financial policy, the establishment of the state's credit on a sound basis. The need for action was obvious: in 1799 the government could obtain credit only with great difficulty and had to pay 3 to 4 per cent interest a month. Bonaparte improved the state's credit by the creation of a sinking fund in the Year IX; although he did not use it to amortize the debt, it did more than any other one thing to raise the national credit. Bonaparte's conception of the importance of state credit and of the means of improving the government's credit rating was an impressive feature of his financial policy.

But Bonaparte felt that one stone was still lacking in his financial arch. During the eighteenth century and the wars of the French Revolution, Great Britain had been able to subsidize its allies because of its credit and the functioning of the Bank of England; this convinced Bonaparte that France, too, needed a national bank. In 1799 French industrialists and merchants were complaining of the difficulty of obtaining credit; they wanted a big bank that would aid them in business. Bonaparte wanted one to support the credit of the government.

The Bank of France, whose statutes were approved on 16 Nivôse, Year VIII (January 6, 1800), was another of Napoleon's outstanding fiscal contributions; one student of economic history calls it one of Napoleon's happiest thoughts. Bonaparte aimed to give the middle classes a source of profit in this privately owned bank, and at the same time provide the government with a source of credit. Initially the Bank had a capital of 30 million francs, divided into shares of a thousand francs each. No matter how many shares a person might own, he could not have more than five votes; but the two hundred largest shareholders elected the Bank's administration—fifteen directors, who in turn chose three of their number to serve as an executive committee, and three censors. Until the 1930's the top two hundred families continued to dominate finance—and thereby to a large extent industry, and on several occasions even the government. Bonaparte used half the capital of the sinking fund to buy stock in the Bank, but it was not enough. The full amount was subscribed only after the best of the few private banks in France, the Bank of Current Accounts, merged with the new Bank.

The Bank of France, in return for surveillance by the government, in 1803 received the exclusive right to issue bank notes for Paris; 500 francs was the smallest denomination. At the same time, the capital of the Bank was increased by 50 per cent. Dividends were limited to 6 per cent; any profits above that figure would have to be invested in government bonds. The Bank helped direct the discount policy of France, deciding the interest rates other banks would charge.

But things went awry shortly after the outbreak of the War of the Third Coalition in 1805. The Bank of France had issued too many notes. People began to convert their notes into cash, in part because of lack of confidence and in part because business slowed down. The Bank ran low on funds. When it announced that only one 1000-franc note per person would be redeemed, there was a financial panic, stimulated by fears of what effect the defeat at Trafalgar would have on the credit of both the state and the Bank. Bank notes lost 10 per cent of their face value.

Napoleon was forced to reorganize the Bank in 1806. Now

it was directly subjected to the government: its statutes had to be approved by Napoleon, who selected a governor and two deputy governors; the Council of State was its judge; a special committee of relations with the Treasury was created, and the government decided whether dividends would be paid. The Bank's capital was doubled to 90 million francs so as to lessen the possibility of any future run on the Bank that might prove disastrous, and its charter was extended from 1818 to 1843. In 1808 the Bank received the right to establish branches, but it set up only three of them—in Lyon, Rouen, and Lille. (The Lille branch lasted only from 1810 to 1813.) The authorization of branches was part of Napoleon's attempt to make truly national a Bank which was so largely Parisian. For instance, its notes circulated and were convertible only in Paris.

Napoleon acted to aid other banks when they experienced financial difficulty, but his policy was not sufficiently liberal to encourage great modern banks. To stimulate industry he tried to keep the interest rate on borrowed money low. Because he often acted without regard to the market, banks were reluctant to lend at the prescribed rate, and men of wealth shied away from the banking field.

Not unnaturally, Napoleon extended his fiscal policy from France to the satellite areas. Naples received a royal bank. In Naples and Tuscany the debt was reduced by partial bankruptcy; in the Papal States it was consolidated at 2 per cent interest. The French tax administration and indirect taxes became the rule in numerous areas—the indirect taxes sometimes, as in Berg and Würzburg, alongside the customary levies. Bavaria made a cadastral survey.

Napoleon took an active part not only in the government's fiscal affairs, but in the economy of the country as a whole. Though he tried to reconcile the war-imposed need for regulation with the liberalism of the *bourgeoisie*, he was not the *laissez-faire* economist the Revolutionaries were. His was rather the outlook and role of an enlightened despot, doing his best to promote, according to his own lights, the welfare of his people. This is why he turned from the Revolutionary, physiocratic idea of unregulated trade to the fixing of prices on meat and bakery items. His natural inclination was to regulate trade by means of corporations,[2] but bankers, industrialists, and the Council of State so generally opposed the idea that freedom of work remained the rule. There were, however, numerous exceptions, particularly in the liberal professions. Bonaparte ordered the prefect of police in Paris to establish trade bodies for baking and butchery; this corporative regime spread to several provincial cities. No person could henceforth enter these trades without authorization from the police. The monopolistic spirit developed rapidly, for the organizations took the medieval guilds as their model. Since they did not have the independence of the guilds, they were really administrative bodies, functioning to serve the state rather than themselves.

Napoleon's actions in the economic field were influenced to a great extent by military and wartime considerations—for example, the problem of feeding his armies. Although he continued so far as possible the Revolutionary practice of having armies live off the land, he also did his best to develop an efficient commissariat. A famous part of his supply system was canned food, particularly meat, for the army. Nicholas Appert had started the food-canning industry in 1804, building a factory that employed fifty people. His method prescribed putting the food in glass jars, which were next carefully stoppered, and then cooked in boiling water for lengths of time varying with the type of food. The navy first used the canned food, with great success even on extended cruises. In 1810 the Minister of the Interior awarded

---

[2] These were not corporations as we use the term today. They were legally established, privileged groups, such as the guilds. Unlike present-day trade unions, the owners of small businesses were the voting members of the guilds.

Appert 12,000 francs on condition he make his process public.

The Continental System and its counterpart, the British blockade, were obviously the most important military elements affecting Napoleon's economic policy. Wanting the Continent to abstain from buying British goods, Napoleon provided as many of them as possible. If that amount proved to be insufficient, the government expended great efforts to promote substitutes for items formerly purchased from the British or obtained from the French colonies (for example, cane sugar) which could no longer be imported. Napoleon encouraged the raising of sugar beets, of cotton, of chicory, of tobacco, and of woad for dyes. The government, in the person of the Minister of the Interior, decided how many acres of a new crop would be planted in a specific department. The prefects then allotted this acreage among the communes.

Although sugar had not long been on European tables, it had become a virtual necessity—or so people thought. Because of the demand, Napoleon offered prizes for a satisfactory method of producing sugar from crops grown in Europe. Grapes seemed to offer a promising possibility; the Ministry of the Interior after 1808 encouraged efforts to derive sugar from grapes in Piedmont and Languedoc, but this never worked out very satisfactorily. Attempts were made to extract sugar from chestnuts, carrots, turnips, and maple trees. The solution finally adopted as the official one was to promote the raising of sugar beets. In 1811, for example, the Minister of the Interior decided that 32,000 hectares (about 80,000 acres) should be planted in sugar beets; in 1812 this figure was raised to 100,000 hectares, almost a quarter of a million acres. In the latter year the Minister of the Interior, Count Jean Montalivet, reported a crop of 98 million kilograms, or about 108,000 tons. Six experimental schools were established to study the growing of sugar beets.

Good quality sugar was extracted from beets early in the Consulate. The Class of Physical and Mathematical Sciences of the

Institute had appointed a commission, which reported on 6 Messidor, Year VIII (June 23, 1800), that beet sugar could supplement cane sugar. But the price of cane sugar was still lower than that of beet sugar, and the Peace of Amiens put an end to efforts to further the production of beet sugar.

Experiments were renewed in 1808. In 1810 Napoleon promised a prize of 600,000 francs for sugar equal in quality and price to cane sugar, and in 1812 the government created five schools to teach beet-sugar refining. The better part of a million francs (woad culture got the rest) was allotted to developing this national industry. The first refineries were built in 1810, and the first commercial beet sugar was produced in the following year, at Lille and Auby. Five hundred licenses were granted for the refining of sugar, with a promise of tax exemption for four years on condition the refinery produced 10,000 kilograms a year. Cane sugar from the Indies could not be imported after 1812 on the ground that it was an English item. But France, refining 7.5 million kilograms (8,250 tons) in 334 factories in 1813, never produced so much beet sugar as Napoleon wanted.

Although all the factories succumbed either during Napoleon's 1814 campaign or after the frontiers were opened, the refining of beet sugar later became one of the most important agricultural industries of France. Beet sugar culture spread to other countries, and today its tonnage far surpasses that of cane sugar in the world at large as well as in France.

Another colonial commodity that the Continent could no longer obtain in sufficient quantities was coffee. Here, too, Napoleon embarked on a policy of trying to locate and perfect a substitute. The most satisfactory one proved to be chicory, which is still drunk in large quantities.

To overcome the shortage of indigo, the government encouraged the manufacture of blue coloring from pastel (woad). A decree of March 15, 1811, stated that 32,000 hectares (almost 80,000 acres) were to be devoted to cultivating woad; that four experimental schools for woad would be created; and that after January 1, 1813, indigo from the Indies would be prohibited. Alsace grew woad quite successfully. Three imperial factories were established in 1813 to manufacture pastel, at Florence, Turin, and Toulouse. Any manufacturer producing 200 kilograms a year was promised premiums and exemption from taxes. Notable progress was made in dyeing, but a prize of 25,000 francs offered in 1810 for a sure and easy method of dyeing wool and silk with Prussian blue went unclaimed.

In general, Napoleon did not control agriculture so closely as he did industry. He did, however, want it improved and encouraged; like the physiocrats, he looked on agriculture as the most important form of economic activity.

Agriculture is the soul, the foundation of the kingdom; industry ministers to the comfort and happiness of the population. Foreign trade is the superabundance; it allows of the exchange of the surplus of agriculture and industry. Foreign trade in its results is infinitely inferior to agriculture; it ought to be the servant of agriculture and home industry.

The support of agriculture took varied forms. Napoleon reestablished a number of fairs which had been interrupted during the Revolution. Jean Chaptal preached and demonstrated the value of organic manure decades before agricultural experts in other countries did so. The government wanted to increase the number of livestock, particularly horses and sheep, as these were the two animals most useful for the army. (An interesting feature of the sheep-raising effort was that the government felt compelled in 1804 to establish a regular wolf-hunting organization.) Not only did Napoleon want more sheep but he wanted better quality. He brought some merino rams from Spain and reestablished the Rambouillet "depot of merinos" that the Revolution had permitted to languish. By the time of the Bourbon restoration French sheep were reputed to be better than the Spanish merinos.

Outside France, Napoleon could not effect agricultural reforms as far-reaching as he would have liked because the *bourgeoisie* was so weak and undeveloped that he had to rely on the aristocracy for officials and therefore could not antagonize it too much. That is why feudal dues, and perhaps even the tithe, in many cases had to be redeemed. Yet attempts were made to bring agriculture up to the French standard. In several places—among them Bavaria, northern Germany, Naples—the common lands were split up, obligatory rotation abolished, and the division of family estates authorized. Since textiles manufactured in Italy could not compete with British and French ones, industrialists and merchants there bought land and applied enlightened economic practices to farming.

Commerce was another area of economic activity that Napoleon encouraged. A significant step was resumption of the practice of holding industrial expositions started by the Directory in 1798. The first exposition held while Bonaparte was in power took place in 1801. That of 1802 was twice as big and showed that the age of machines was approaching. Charles James Fox, the English Whig leader, visited the 1802 exposition while negotiating the Treaty of Amiens and admired the riches on display. The most important exposition, and the only one held during the Empire, took place in 1806; more than 1,400 exhibitors displayed their wares. Textiles particularly distinguished themselves, followed by metal products. Ever since Napoleon's day, industrial expositions have been an important sales tool.

The most notable institutional innovation in the field of commerce was the establishment of chambers of commerce in numerous towns. A few chambers of commerce (which in France had an official character) had existed under the *ancien régime*, but they had disappeared in 1791. A decree of 3 Nivôse, Year XI (December 23, 1803), re-established twenty-two of them. The official nature of the chambers meant that they were established only where the government thought they would be useful. Every department had at least one, but there might be as many as one per *arrondissement*. They were consultative bodies, giving the government advice and information on commercial and industrial facts and interests, and on public works and transportation facilities, so as to increase commercial prosperity. By so doing they helped the government shape its economic policy. The membership of a chamber might range from five to fifteen, selected by co-optation for six-year terms from among merchants, financiers, manufacturers, and masters of coasting vessels.

The most important long-range contribution the Napoleonic period made to commerce was the improvement of transportation. Even though Napoleon built or improved roads for purposes more military than economic, they did facilitate commerce. Particularly was this true of the roads built in the Alps. During his fifteen years in power, Napoleon built or repaired 40,000 miles of roads. Not all of them were imperial routes; many were farm-to-market roads. At the end of his reign there were 33,000 kilometers of royal roads; 30,000 kilometers were open, but, in part as a result of the Allied invasion of France, only 12,000 were in good condition. Napoleon also built bridges, including four over the Seine at Paris and one over the Rhine at Kehl.

Although he created a service of Bridges and Highways, many roads and bridges were poorly maintained, and on occasion Napoleon had to fall back on the *corvée,* unpaid compulsory work on the roads, because public funds were lacking. Yet only with Napoleon's greater resources and better-managed finances was there a sizable budget for roads and bridges.

The government also tried to perfect a system of canals that would provide cheap transportation for bulky items. Napoleon completed the canals of the Center and of St. Quentin, resumed work on and finished the Ourcq canal, and worked on several others, including one from the Rhone to the Rhine. In all he increased the existing 1,000 kilometers of canals by 20 per cent.

In spite of these accomplishments, however, the lack of adequate transportation between France and the other European countries was a major factor contributing to Napoleon's inability to substitute French industry for British. Even though the roads existed, the transportation they afforded was so slow and expensive as seriously to limit the potential market in the rest of Europe. France was able to export profitably only items with a high value-per-weight ratio. The canals and rivers in general did not run in directions that would be of most use. (The Rhone-Rhine canal was an exception.) The only possible way to carry on large-scale trade without a long period of preparation was by means of coastal shipping, which became more difficult as the years passed.

As we have already noted, Napoleon thought foreign commerce was less significant than agriculture and industry, but that did not prevent his giving attention to it. A law of April 30, 1806, established a new tariff schedule, which remained the basis of the general French tariff until 1881. This schedule made importation of cotton cloth almost impossible. In 1810 the French government usurped all foreign trade for itself. Napoleon's direction of foreign trade set a precedent followed by 20th-century dictatorships.

At least two of Napoleon's codes furthered commerce. The Civil Code encouraged merchants by assuring them that no new restrictions would be put on trade. The Commercial Code, which went into effect on New Year's Day of 1808, dealt with commerce in general, maritime commerce, bankruptcies, and commercial jurisdiction. Although it did not fully meet the needs of the day (in part because it relied heavily on Colbert's commercial ordinance of 1673 and marine ordinance of 1681), the mere fact of codification and uniformity of rules and laws simplified the carrying-on of trade.

Imposing the decimal system on a nationwide scale in March of 1803 further simplified and stimulated commerce. The Convention had adopted the system, but application of it had proceeded slowly. In some of the areas that he subjected Napoleon abolished internal tariffs. Bavaria further facilitated its domestic commerce by adopting a uniform system of weights and measures.

France for the first time received a specifically economic ministry. The Ministry of Manufactures and Commerce, established in 1811, began to function in 1812 with Jean Chaptal as its first chief. One of its duties was to organize exhibitions; earlier the Ministry of the Interior had handled this task. This economic ministry also distributed financial aid to new industries. Chaptal, for instance, had 62 million francs at his disposal to encourage the silk, cotton and iron industries. The chemical industry made soda a common product. The production of luxury items, especially silk stuffs, was re-established. In 1806 rather good red lead was produced, and there was hope that France might no longer have to pay tribute for it to Holland and England.

Napoleon especially attempted to foster industry in France, which suffered more than the rest of Europe from the Continental System; industrial prosperity began to decline three years after the Berlin Decree. Tariffs, subsidies to new industries, and governmental intervention were the most important means of favoring industry. Tariffs protected the French textile industry against Swiss competition. Napoleon considered the Belgian departments to be economically, as well as politically, an integral part of France—this may be one reason for the rapid industrialization of Belgium after the Napoleonic period. French factories, even though unprotected by tariffs, were able to withstand Belgian competition. Other areas incorporated into the French Empire were kept outside the French customs system. Some of the satellite states adopted highly protective tariffs of their own.

A strong motive for stimulating industry was that Napoleon feared the impact of unemployment on the attitude of the masses, and on his own popularity. On one occasion he stated,

"I fear insurrections based on a lack of bread; I should fear less a battle of 200,000 men." His early popularity, particularly in Paris, rested on his providing food, at low prices, and work. More stringent enforcement of the draft laws contributed to reducing the unemployment rate. The government, in February of 1804, authorized placement bureaus so long as they were not organized by either the workers or the employers. In general, the bureaus were the creatures of the municipalities. When French industry faced a crisis in the winter of 1806–07, Napoleon loaned manufacturers 6 million francs at a maximum interest rate of 2 per cent. Designedly, it was the great industrialists who benefited most: they were the ones employing large numbers of workers who, if unemployed, might become revolutionary in their thinking. There was so little unemployment during the whole Napoleonic period, mainly because of the wars, that large numbers of women and children were hired in industry.

Napoleon desired to build up the textile industry. Mechanical spinning was almost unknown in France during the Revolution, but there may have been as many as a million spindles by 1812.[3] Production rose between 1806 and 1808 from 2 to 4.5 million kilograms. Because France could not trade with the Far East, it learned to make percales, muslins, calico. Both fashion and economy made printed cotton cloth preferable to silk. Cotton manufacturers became the most ardent protectionists in France.

But the Continental System worked at cross purposes with Napoleon's aim. Cotton manufacturers suffered from a severe shortage of raw cotton. Napoleon therefore advocated cotton farming in southern France, Italy, and Corsica, only to have all the attempts fail. When he discovered that not all the necessary raw material could be produced on the Continent, he granted to manufacturers, who paid for the privilege, licenses for the importation, but a tariff was to be paid on all imports. (At least the Treasury might benefit from an economic necessity!) Yet he

[3] Statistics of the time are unreliable. The number was between 700,000 and 1,000,000.

took a dislike to the cotton industry and even banned cotton goods from the imperial palaces in 1811. He gladly loaned money to cotton manufacturers who switched to some other product, and he offered a prize of a million francs to anybody inventing a machine to spin linen. Such a machine was invented in 1810, but Napoleon reneged on his promise.

Except for cotton textiles, the blockade stimulated local industrial production, profiting from the prohibition of British goods elsewhere in Europe. Even French exports did not affect the industry of importing countries too severely, because lack of adequate and cheap transportation kept the French goods from being competitive in price. But the war hurt industrial progress on the Continent. The port cities and their manufactures, dependent on shipping for sales, were ruined. Since industrial advance in general depended on English machinery, it would have been more rapid if Englishmen had been able to continue to install it.

The government tried to make use of machinery more widespread. As early as 1802, during the period of peace after Amiens, France introduced machinery to make cloth and found it to be far more economical than manual labor. Liéven Bauwens introduced English methods of cotton manufacture into Belgium. (The British brought action against him in the Court of King's Bench, which condemned him to death in absentia.)

Printing of cloth by means of rollers became widespread during the Empire. Although Napoleon's government cannot take credit for the Jacquard loom, it did reward the inventor. Joseph Jacquard received a bronze medal at the exposition of 1801. Two years later he was attached to the Conservatory of Arts and Crafts at Paris, and in 1804 he received a gold medal from the Society for the Encouragement of National Industry. In 1806 his invention became public property; in return the government awarded him an annual pension of 3,000 francs and a royalty of fifty francs on each machine. By 1812 there were 11,000 Jacquard looms in France.

Another way in which Napoleon promoted industrial growth

was by the establishment or reorganization of technical schools. The one technical school in France in 1789 had almost ceased to function during the Revolution. In 1800 Bonaparte transferred it from Liancourt to Compiègne; it became one of the three schools in the *Prytanée français*.[4] In 1803 it was changed into a "School of Arts and Crafts," and the curriculum was revised. In 1806 it was moved to its present location, at Châlons-sur-Marne. Each year between one hundred and two hundred students, at least eight years old, enrolled for a six-year academic and practical course. Napoleon opened two other technical schools, at Beaupréau and Trier, and planned still others. In addition, he greatly developed the Conservatory of Arts and Crafts established by the National Convention in 1794, re-established the school of dyeing at the Gobelin factory, and founded schools of mines.

Napoleon intervened in mining more than in any other economic activity, in part because it had been subject to government control for half a century. He did not initiate anything but merely developed the regulations and brought them up to date. New regulations were necessary because the Mines Law of 1791 and the Civil Code contradicted each other. A new Mines Law of 1810 classified mines as quarries, open-sky mines, or underground mines. A landowner might exploit a quarry as he pleased. For an open-sky mine he needed official authorization; in addition, a neighborhood ironworks could, against the landowner's will, exploit an open mine in return for compensation to the landowner. (Such a factory's actions would be in the interest of the state.) The right to mine underground was granted only by an act of the government; the concession was permanent and transmissible. This system created a veritable feudality of ironmasters with mines as their baronial estates. An "Imperial Body of Mines" was created seven months after passage of the Mines

[4] This is treated in more detail in the discussion of education in Chapter VII.

Act. Its inspector-general formed a "General Council of Mines" to deliver advisory opinions on demands for concessions; its engineers made sure that safety regulations were applied.

Although the Napoleonic Code provided for legal equality in most cases, it did not do so for the relations of workers and employers. In court the word of an employer was always accepted in a controversy with a worker. Napoleon kept in force the Revolutionary legislation against association, with the penalties prescribed for workers who broke the law being far harsher than those for employers. The provision of any punishment at all for employers was, however, a Napoleonic addition to the Le Chapelier law of 1791.

The first Napoleonic law dealing with relations between masters and workers was enacted on 22 Germinal, Year XI (April 11, 1803). This law required workers to carry a labor workbook (*livret*) so that any future employer might know about their previous employment; the *livret* did not, however, contain any comments on the employee's ability or loyalty. A worker minus his *livret* was considered a vagabond and was liable to six months in prison. One of the more baleful institutions that persisted from the Napoleonic period, the workbook lasted until 1890.

The same law of 1803 charged mayors (in Paris, the prefect of police) with the settlement of differences between owners and employees, but these officials proved to be more suitable for repressing disorders than for conciliating disputes. It also provided for the protection of trademarks and the establishment of consultative chambers. Henceforth the large cities could have chambers for manufactures, factories, arts and crafts. Each chamber would be composed of six manufacturers and be presided over by the mayor.

Despite his making the worker legally inferior to the employer, Napoleon established councils of *prud'hommes* (wise men, or skilled men), representing both groups, to advise and rule on

117

working conditions. The first council resulted from a request by the chamber of commerce of Lyons as Napoleon was passing through that city on his way to Italy in 1805. The law that established it on March 18, 1806, authorized the council to settle employer-worker disputes involving not more than sixty francs; if the amount was greater, the council was merely to try to effect a conciliation. Another decree, of June 1, 1809, laid down in greater detail how councils would be established in the future. It extended the council's jurisdiction to amounts greater than sixty francs; but if more was involved, the decision was subject to appeal. After 1810 no sum under 100 francs could be appealed. By this time the institution had spread to twenty-six cities. The procedure for establishment of a council was as follows: the chamber of commerce petitioned the prefect; he relayed the request to the Minister of the Interior; and the central government made the final decision. Each council, based as it was on the principle of specialization, had jurisdiction over only one industry in one locality. In Lyon, this was the silk industry.

Ranging in number from five to fifteen, the members of a council were elected by assemblies called and presided over by the prefect. Those eligible to participate were employers who had been in business six years and literate workers with six years of seniority who could afford to pay for patents. Although superficially the election process was democratic, the eligibility requirements for the workers eliminated most of them as candidates or voters. On the councils the management had more representatives than did the workers throughout the Napoleonic period and for some time thereafter. Representation was not even so nearly equal as appeared on paper to be the case, for—to use Lyons as an example—the workers were represented by foremen, with not a single plain worker on the council.

Not all the members had to hear each dispute; only one employer and one employee member were necessary to conciliate minor quarrels; two thirds at least had to hear and decide issues on violations of laws or policing of industry. To fall within the jurisdiction of a council of *prud'hommes*, a dispute had to stem directly from the industrial situation. The most common types of cases handled were wage disputes and charges of mistreatment of workers. The *prud'hommes* also dealt with breaches of contract. If conciliation failed, the issue was referred to a so-called board of judgment, really a board of arbitration. The councils could impose fines and jail sentences of up to three months.

The councils were also to maintain property rights in trademarks and new industrial designs (as in textiles), and to inspect the workshops twice a year—but only after giving two days' notice to the employer. In addition they had jurisdiction over some simple police matters.

Through the councils of *prud'hommes* France became the first modern state to have a court for industry. They played an important role because they were vital, useful, and fair. The workers obtained speedy justice; the conciliation boards met at least every other day, the arbitration boards at least once a week. As the workers paid no fees, justice was also cheap. Not the least of the virtues of the councils was their simplicity and informality, especially suitable for this type of activity.

An early attempt at satisfactory management-labor relations in the new era of industrialization, these councils of *prud'hommes* were one of the wisest institutions the Empire bestowed on industry—and one of the most durable. Though they have become less important with the rise of labor unions, they still exist in France, in a form somewhat modified in the course of the 19th century. Seven other countries in Europe adopted the institution. Various German states, led by Prussia in 1846, instituted such councils before they were made compulsory in 1901 for all German communities with more than 20,000 inhabitants. Austria-Hungary adopted the institution in 1869, Spain in 1873, Switzerland in 1885, Portugal and Belgium (the latter for the second time) both in 1889, and Italy in 1893.

Historians differ as to whether Napoleon was responsible for many innovations in the economic field. This much can be asserted. Napoleon could have unified the commerce of Italy, and he could have established a German *Zollverein* (customs union); these steps he refused to take for political reasons. He envisioned a Continental market merely to enhance the position of France, not for its own sake. But his legislation, taken as a whole, signified considerable progress. Napoleon favored capitalism by continuing in France and extending to other areas such Revolutionary reforms as freedom of work, the abolition of serfdom and feudal burdens, the suppression of internal customs and tolls, uniform weights and measures, and the possibility of converting land into movable property. The Bank of France, the chambers of commerce, the incipient industrial courts all contributed to the same end. Even the Continental System protected infant industries. Though Napoleon exaggerated when he said that he "created" French industry, he did much to foster it.

·VI·

RELATIONS WITH THE CHURCH

Napoleon's attitude toward religion was much like that of the enlightened despots. His tolerance for religion, as theirs, stemmed partly from his contempt for it. "I was Mohammedan in Egypt, I shall be Catholic here, for the good of the people. I don't believe in religions." A month before his death he commented, "I am glad I have no religion. It is a great consolation. I have no imaginary fears, no fear of the future." Yet he realized the tremendous support that religion might give to his regime. As he once trenchantly said, "Men who do not believe in God—one does not govern them, one shoots them." He felt that one shortcoming of the French Revolutionaries had been their failure to utilize religious sentiment for their own interests.

The Revolutionaries had at first adopted a dual policy, which Napoleon thought proper, permitting greater religious tolerance in accordance with the Declaration of the Rights of Man, but subjecting the church to the state by suppressing the monasteries and by adopting a Civil Constitution of the Clergy, which made the church a branch of the state. The Protestants and Jews, the latter in two stages, received the same civil rights enjoyed by the Catholics.

121

THE NAPOLEONIC REVOLUTION

Two important factors motivated the National Assembly when it took these actions: the need for financial backing, and the fact that at least the upper clergy was anti-Revolutionary. The King had had the right to nominate bishops; in 1789 only one of 135 was a commoner. The King also had named the heads of three fifths of the monasteries and convents. Aristocratic lords chose many of the parish priests, but the upper and lower clergy had little in common except doctrine.

There were other aspects of the religious situation in 1789 which were not to the liking of the Revolutionaries. Although the clergy was declining in numbers and constituted only about one half of one per cent of the population, a total of 70,000 secular clergy and 60,000 regular clergy seemed excessive. Everybody was liable for paying the tithe (in actual practice it fell most heavily on the peasants), which brought in about three fifths of the church's total income of 200 million francs, of which roughly four fifths went to the upper clergy. The value of the real property of the church approached 4 billion francs. The church also, the Revolutionaries felt, played too large a part in such aspects of a person's life as his education and marriage. Protestants and Jews, whose combined numbers made up less than 5 per cent of the population, had no rights.

During the period of the Convention, dechristianization, though never fully carried out, became an official policy. Churches became Temples of Reason; Robespierre, who believed in freedom of religion, sponsored a deistic Worship of the Supreme Being. Following his fall, the Revolutionaries disestablished the Roman Catholic Church and proclaimed religious liberty.

The policy of the Convention had been continued by the Directory, which, in its last two years, had sponsored (though not financially) official religions which involved a glorification of the Revolutionary regime. A civil religion it sponsored held its "worship services" on the *décadi*, the three rest days per month which in the republican calendar had replaced Sundays. Some intellectuals independently sponsored theophilanthropy, a rational, civic cult based on man's obligation to society. For a time the government supported it. But none of these cults had a large following; the statutory provision for freedom of worship merely allowed a revival of Catholicism, which the Directory then proceeded to persecute. At the time of Bonaparte's coup the Catholic Church was still separated from the state and still divided. The nonjuring (or refractory) clergy, who had refused to take the oath demanded by the Civil Constitution of the Clergy, had largely gone into hiding or been expelled; the juring (or constitutional) clergy were preaching to empty pews.

Two elements in the religious situation were intolerable to Bonaparte. The existence of several different religions was the first—an impossible situation to a despot desiring a classical type of unity and centralization in the state. The other was the separation of church and state.

Bonaparte felt strongly that "religion must be in the hands of the state." To his mind a policy of separation left too many problems unsolved, too many questions unanswered; among these were the authority of a foreign pope over a French clergy, confiscated church property, and the constitutional clergy. Only if religion was legally organized could there be assurance of systematic surveillance over it.

His remarks to the Council of State in 1800 illustrate why he thought religion could not be permitted to develop free of governmental control: "I don't see in religion the mystery of the incarnation, but the mystery of the social order. It ties up to heaven an idea of equality which prevents the rich from being massacred by the poor." He repeated the same thought on other occasions:

Society cannot exist without inequality of fortunes, and inequality of fortunes cannot exist without religion. When a man is dying of hunger alongside another who stuffs himself, it is impossible to make him accede to the difference unless there is an authority which says to him, "God wishes it thus; there must be some poor and some rich in the world, but hereafter and for all eternity the division will be made differently."

Bonaparte took steps as early as the time of his second campaign in Italy to effect unity within the Catholic religion and to obtain the backing of the clergy. He undertook negotiations with the newly elected Pope Pius VII for the purpose of arriving at a concordat, or religious agreement. First the Pope had to promise not to permit British goods to enter his ports in the Papal States. Pius was glad to negotiate because he feared, after a century of skepticism and a decade of revolution, that the church in France was on the verge of being dissolved.

During the negotiations for the Concordat, the Pope insisted on the end of theophilanthropy, whose adherents wanted to use the churches simultaneously with the Catholics. Bonaparte was more than willing to oblige the Pope; he had already ended official support of such cults. In October 1801 he issued a decree which forbade the theophilanthropists to meet in public buildings and thus effectively ended their movement.

Bonaparte had earlier taken several other measures that encouraged a rebirth of Catholicism. Three decrees issued 7 Nivôse, Year VIII (December 28, 1799), were of particular importance. They permitted churches to be open every day, ordered that all non-alienated churches be used for religious purposes, and required from the clergy merely an oath of loyalty to the Constitution rather than one expressing hatred for monarchy. As a result of this last decree, many *émigré* clergy felt free to return to France.

Without any formal action by the government, Sunday again had come to be a day of rest. In June of 1800 a decree stated it was no longer obligatory to observe the *décadi*. (A police report in that month stated, however, that the *décadi* were celebrated calmly and that the priests had no influence on this point.)

The chief aim of Bonaparte in working for a concordat was to remove the church as a source of opposition to his regime. As he remarked, "Fifty *émigré* bishops in England's pay are the present leaders of the French clergy. Their influence must be destroyed, and for this I must have the authority of the Pope." If he could reach a general understanding with the Pope, the royalists would no longer have any clerical reason to oppose him. Bonaparte considered religious pacification as more than desirable—as indispensable. With it he might achieve pacification of the Vendée, the scene of a royalist- and Catholic-inspired uprising, and hasten the submission of such newly annexed, staunchly Catholic territories as Belgium, Piedmont, and the Rhineland. As there had been a Catholic renaissance even before he came to power, Bonaparte also thought that a concordat would be a popular measure.

Bonaparte approached the negotiations for a concordat in the spirit of Gallicanism, which held that the church in France had ecclesiastical liberties of its own, independent of the jurisdiction of the Pope. Gallicanism had received its most explicit statement in the Declaration of Gallican Liberties, drawn up by the bishops of France in 1682, during the reign of Louis XIV. The Declaration had stated that the Pope's word was not final, that a general council of the church was superior to the Pope, that his decrees would not go into effect in France until approved by a council of French bishops, and that they should not contain anything in violation of the ancient traditions and conventions of the French church.

Since Bonaparte wanted the church in France to serve the state, there could be no foreign meddling, not even from the Vatican. However, his kind of Gallicanism—not unknown to the Bourbon monarchy—would approve of domestic meddling; it permitted the state to intervene in worship activities, and thus in the government of the church.

The Concordat was finally arranged in 1801, even though it was not published until the spring of 1802; and even at the latter date it was hidden behind news of the Treaty of Amiens, as Bonaparte felt that Revolutionary sentiment was strong enough to produce an outcry against it. His analysis was correct. The masses welcomed the free exercise of public worship, but the intellectual world was at best indifferent and at worst hostile. A police report made to Bonaparte a few days after the proclamation stated that authors and even members of the Institute were worried and were afraid to write because the "religious system prevails, they fear the priests and their vengeance and want to keep their heads."[1] The opposition of the Tribunate and the Legislative Body was one reason Bonaparte revamped them in the Year X. The Institute and Sieyès were likewise opposed; Sieyès' opposition led to his political decline.

Also antagonistic was the Republican army. One general remarked to Bonaparte concerning the proclamation of the Concordat on the day before Easter, "That's a fine stupid sermon; all that is lacking is the hundred thousand men who died to suppress all that." Other generals showed their hostility the next day by pulling the priests out of their seats at the church services. The resistance was so strong that the Prussian minister reported home, "Of all the operations which Bonaparte has carried through, that of the legal re-establishment of religion is the one which has most exercised all the constancy of his will and all the resources of his mind."

The resistance of the *idéologues* was hardly warranted. Napoleon was not giving up all the gains of the Revolution in his approach; instead, he was in many respects guaranteeing them against ecclesiastical attack. For example, one of the major issues to be decided by the negotiators was the disposition of lands confiscated from the Catholic Church early in the Revolution. Bonaparte had no thought of appeasing His Holiness by sacrificing the support of the peasants who had purchased this land.

[1] For a discussion of the Institute, see Chapter VII.

The Concordat therefore stipulated that all former Church property purchased by individuals would remain theirs.[2] The Pope could not, however, agree that the property had changed hands rightfully, as to do so would be to deny the papal tradition; hence the Concordat merely stated that there would be no attempt to dispossess the new owners.

Perhaps the issue most bothersome to the Pope was that of the juring clergy, those who had sworn to abide by the Civil Constitution of the Clergy. He did not recognize them as performing clerical functions, but considered them rebels who should be ousted from office. On this issue a compromise was worked out. All the clergy were to resign their posts, to be replaced by new nominees. For Bonaparte, this was the easiest way to break the resistance of the bishops, both the refractory and the constitutional. (He did not trust some of the latter because he thought they were too democratic.) Resignation of the juring clergy could be arranged easily, for that was a political matter. But never before in history had the Pope forced clergy to resign. Of the ninety-three bishops who had been consecrated prior to the Revolution, only fifty-five agreed to give up their posts. The other thirty-eight became refractory in a new sense, refusing to obey the Pope. Righteously aggrieved, they felt the Pope had poorly rewarded their loyalty to the Papacy during the Revolutionary years. When he struck them off the episcopal list, after five months, some of them formed a "Little Church," which came to an end only in the 1890's, during the pontificate of Leo XIII.

The new members of the clergy were to be nominated by the government, in the person of the First Consul, and only then to be consecrated by the Pope. This, plus the fact that the government would pay their salaries, meant that the clergy were to be

---

[2] This clause was in harmony with the provision in the Constitution of the Year VIII that holders of national property would not be disturbed in their possession.

largely under the control of the state. Bonaparte created a "General Direction of Religion" in the Ministry of the Interior on October 7, 1801, and appointed Jean Portalis to head it; in 1804 it became the Ministry for Ecclesiastical Affairs. Bonaparte's action in assuming authority over the church was in the same "enlightened" tradition as the Civil Constitution of the Clergy a dozen years earlier.

Twelve constitutional bishops, ten of whom would not retract their earlier oath to the Civil Constitution of the Clergy, were among Bonaparte's appointees. The Pope did not install them until they retracted two years later, since he was not bound by any time limit to approve the government's nominees. By an agreement reached in 1811 the Pope conceded that if he did not confer investiture within six months, the metropolitan could do so, but only "expressly in the name of the sovereign pontiff," in order that the latter might annul it. No bishopric was to remain vacant for more than a year. Nomination, investiture, and consecration were all to take place within this period of time.

The Concordat further laid down the principle that there would be a new delimitation of dioceses. The Pope knew that Bonaparte wanted to reduce the number of bishops in order that each, having a larger area to oversee, would be less able to supervise in detail the developments in his diocese. The Organic Articles (discussed below) stated that there would be sixty bishops, including ten archbishops, about three thousand parishes (which in principle were to coincide with cantons), and as many chapels as necessary. In practice each canton had one priest and each commune at least one chapel served by a minister. The distinction between parish priests (*curés*) and ministers (*desservants*), whereby the former supervised the latter, was new and canonically indefensible; Bonaparte adopted it for financial reasons and because there was a shortage of priests. Pay ranged from lodging alone for ministers to 15,000 francs for archbishops.

Another major issue was whether the Catholic Church would

be the official state religion. Bonaparte, heeding Talleyrand (a former bishop), declared that he could not accept an affirmative decision as it would be contrary to the ideas of the Revolution. The papal negotiators therefore agreed to a statement that Catholicism was the religion of the great majority of French citizens, in return for the consuls' agreeing personally to make a "private confession" of Catholicism.

The Concordat also provided that the Roman Catholic Church might once again receive bequests and endowments and that the bishops could once again control churches necessary for worship. The Holy See had to recognize the French Republic. Thus were the main issues resolved.

Bonaparte inserted into the Concordat one statement whose importance was not generally recognized at the time, though Cardinal Consalvi, the Papal Secretary of State, argued against it in vain; later it became the source of many difficulties between the Pope and Napoleon. This was a clause that the French government was permitted to issue such police regulations for religion as were deemed necessary. Napoleon interpreted this statement as authorization for issuing Organic Articles for the Catholic Religion at the same time that the Concordat was published. These Organic Articles enabled the state to exercise close supervision not only over the current status of the church, but over its future development as well.

They provided, among other things, that the government had to approve all regulations for seminaries, which were to have exclusively French teachers and profess the principles of the Gallican Liberties. No papal bull or other communication could enter France without the approval of the government, which also had to approve any papal legate to France.

It looked very much from the Organic Articles as though Bonaparte had not only gone back to France's Revolutionary origins, but had reverted to the days of the absolute monarchy as well. The Pope not unnaturally felt that he had been tricked and deceived; but his attitude toward the Organic Articles was one of protesting acquiescence, as he did not want to disturb the new religious peace.

The Organic Articles also specified that there would be only one catechism for all of France. Superficially this seemed like a sound idea, but the catechism was not completed until after Napoleon had assumed the title of Emperor, and he used it for propaganda purposes. A section written at his dictation, to put the church even more at the service of the state, included the following:

Q. What are the duties of Christians with respect to the princes who govern them, and what are in particular our duties toward Napoleon I, our Emperor?

A. . . . love, respect, obedience, fidelity, military service, tributes ordered for the preservation and defense of the Empire and of his throne; we also owe him fervent prayers for his safety and for the spiritual and temporal prosperity of the State.

Q. Why do we have these duties towards our Emperor?

A. First, by bountifully bestowing talents on our Emperor both in peace and war, God has established him as our sovereign and has made him the minister of His power and His image on earth. To honor and serve our Emperor is therefore to honor and serve God himself. Secondly, because our Lord Jesus Christ . . . has taught us what we owe to our sovereign . . . ; He has ordered us to give to Caesar what belongs to Caesar.

Q. Are there not special motives which must attach us more strongly to Napoleon, our Emperor?

A. Yes; for he is the one whom God has given us in difficult times to re-establish the public worship of the holy religion of our fathers and to be the protector of it. He has re-established and maintained public order by his profound and active wisdom; he defends the State with his powerful arm; he has become the Lord's anointed through the consecration which he received from the pontifical sovereign, head of the universal Church.

Q. What must one think of those who may fail in their duty toward our Emperor?

A. According to the apostle Paul, they would resist the established order of God himself and would be worthy of eternal damnation.

Q. Do the duties toward our Emperor bind us equally towards his successors?

A. Yes, undoubtedly; for we read in the Holy Scripture that God, Lord of heaven and earth, . . . gives empires not only to one person in particular, but also to his family.

Though forced upon the church, this section met surprisingly little resistance.

This was only one of the many ways in which Napoleon demanded that the Catholic Church be a support to his regime. Portalis, in Prairial of Year X, shortly after the proclamation of the Concordat, told the archbishops that the government expected all ministers to work to unite the citizens; to inspire a love for laws, respect for social institutions, and obedience to the magistrates; and to direct grateful piety to the prosperity of the Republic and the welfare of the people.

Having been careful as to the bishops he nominated (though he could not always be sure of controlling them after their consecration), Bonaparte felt free to call on them to issue pastoral letters, which the parish priests would read from the pulpit at every service, on matters useful to the government. The government gave the bishops the outline for the letters and censored them before they were circulated among the clergy. As Napoleon told Portalis in 1807, "No bishop ever dared not heed these recommendations." In fact, some of the bishops were so effulgent that their charges to their clergy sounded like the beginning of the Napoleonic legend. They in effect became auxiliaries of the police and promised to pass on to the government anything they might hear which was prejudicial to it.

From time to time the clergy also read Napoleon's bulletins in part or in full from the pulpit; but Napoleon, ever fearful of the clergy, was never sure what its role should be with respect to these pieces. In 1805, for example, he wrote his Minister of Police, Joseph Fouché:

I see difficulties on the subject of reading bulletins in the churches. I don't find this reading expedient; it is suitable only to give more importance to the priests than they should have, for it gives them the right to comment, and, where there is bad news, they will not fail to do so.

Everybody loves pomp and circumstance, perhaps most of all those people who will never have any in their own behalf. The church could satisfy these classes by having a *Te Deum* sung to celebrate such occasions as victories or important events in Napoleon's life. The religious connotation of the *Te Deum* had an impact on the simple folk, who, according to the police, were further impressed and moved by the accompanying music. Appropriate speeches were also given on these occasions, to the benefit of the government.

The arrangements accepted at the time of the Concordat, though not completely satisfactory to either party, lasted more than a hundred years in France, being abrogated only in 1905. Bonaparte had thus effected a long-term solution of the grievous problem of church-state relationships—a monumental achievement. After 1905 the Catholic Church had the same status as other churches; the main change was that the state no longer paid the clergy or nominated the bishops.

Superficially it would seem that Bonaparte had been the great beneficiary of the Concordat and its corollary Organic Articles. There is no denying his gains; he obtained exactly what he wanted. He severed the ties of the church to the *ancien régime;* the church as an independent state within the state was gone forever, the clergy could no longer be considered a separate social order. The average Frenchman was pleased, the Catholic clergy in annexed territories were calmed. But Napoleon's gains were immediate and practical.

In the long run the Papacy secured the more important benefits. The Catholic Church, in mortal danger in France, once again obtained a legal foothold. Despite Bonaparte's Gallicanism, the provision that the Pope could dispossess consecrated bishops gave the Pope more power over the clergy in France than he had ever held during the *ancien régime,* and more power over bishops. Only with the ecumenical council of the 1960's was there evidence of a reversal of the trend toward increasing subordination of the episcopacy to the Papacy.

The Concordat made no mention of the regular clergy (i.e., members of religious orders), probably because Bonaparte in 1801 considered them too insignificant to be a matter of concern; yet at the very time of negotiating the Concordat he was authorizing the first post-Revolutionary religious orders, especially for nursing sisters. Religious orders that bound their members by permanent vows remained forbidden, and all others had to be specifically authorized by the government. By 1810 there were over two hundred nursing or teaching congregations of women and some missionary orders for men. Omission of any mention of the regular clergy in the Concordat meant that when religious orders were authorized, they owed their allegiance to the Pope directly, rather than through the bishops as intermediaries. Absence of any clause on the monastic orders was the origin of strife between them and the state in the Third Republic.

From the Concordat the Catholic Church also gained financial advantages, and an end to the schism in the church. (Both Bonaparte and the Pope wanted this last item.) The bishops gained the right of naming curés and priests, a right they did not possess under the *ancien régime;* until 1790 noble lords had held the patronage of parish churches.

Finally, the conflict between Napoleon and the Pope over the Organic Articles defeated part of Napoleon's purpose in agreeing to the Concordat. The clergy tended to support the Pope; the government once again faced a clerical opposition. In 1811 Napoleon wrote Eugène de Beauharnais, his adopted son and viceroy of the Kingdom of Italy, of his "pronounced intention to put an end to this scandalous struggle of the priesthood against

133

my authority." Subsequently a new concordat was signed in 1813, but the Pope shortly denounced it.

Napoleon's insistence on state control of the church by its very excess turned many moderate clerics into ultramontanists. The lower clergy became ultramontanist, adopting this exaggerated view of papal supremacy as a protective device against close subjection to the state and the bishops. Both the advantages secured by the Papacy and its apparent defeat contributed to the ultramontanism of the 19th century and the eventual proclamation of the dogma of papal infallibility in 1870.

It was political rather than ecclesiastical affairs, however, which caused the greatest difficulty between Napoleon and Pius VII, and which led to the arrest of the Pope in 1808 and his subsequent detention, first at Grenoble and then at Savona. Such treatment of the head of the church heightened opposition to Napoleon in deeply Catholic countries; it was, for instance (far more than any feeling of nationalism), a major factor in the ferocity of the Spanish fighting. The rupture with the Pope also made a tremendous impression on Belgium and the Rhineland, where ultramontanism was strong. The Papacy now became the object of an unwonted sympathy.

Likewise important in Spain was the suppression of two thirds of the monasteries and of ecclesiastical endowments. Wherever French authority extended, Napoleon reduced the number of monasteries and tried to secularize the government, as had been done in France during the Revolution. There was, however, no uniformity of such action in the various regions. In Berg secularization affected only a few chapters of monastic orders; in Baden almost all the convents were closed, and the property of the Catholic clergy was secularized; in Westphalia, all the chapters and convents were suppressed, and their property was sequestered and sold. In Frankfurt religious marriage remained obligatory. The Papal States did not become a secular society. The inhabitants of the Kingdom of Italy disliked the reduction in the number of parishes and the limitation placed on the number of seminarians. In the Illyrian Provinces the number of dioceses was reduced and the ecclesiastical tithe abolished. In some places, such as southern Germany, these reforms tended to last; in others, such as Spain, they merely added fuel to the flames of hostility already burning bright. Napoleon looked like a religious revolutionary in other countries, while in France he was partly a continuer of the religious policy of the French Revolution and partly a reactionary.

Napoleon's treatment of the Protestants in France resembled that given the Catholics. His policy was in keeping with the tradition of religious toleration found in the Enlightenment.

The Protestants were regulated by their own Organic Articles, forty-four in number as compared with seventy-seven for the Catholics. Separate organizational arrangements were made for Calvinists and Lutherans because of their differing beliefs and histories. Those for the Calvinists contradicted their democratic church organization by letting the rich members run the churches and by giving the ministers unprecedented authority. Protestant seminaries were controlled in the same strict manner as were those of the Catholics. The government named all the seminary teachers, and had to approve all doctrinal decisions or disciplinary changes before they could be published or taught. Protestant ministers, paid by the state, were expected to pray for the republic and the consuls. Only French nationals, who were forbidden to have relations with any foreign authority, could be ministers. But the Protestants did not protest the regulations; they were too pleased with the official recognition. This recognition extended to areas outside France. In Baden all Christians had enjoyed religious toleration before this time; now Württemberg also granted it. In Bavaria the last restrictions on Protestants were lifted in 1809, and in the next year the Protestants by edict received an official organization. The same decree let people change religions and suppressed the obligatory financial support of the Catholic Church.

Napoleon treated the Jews less as a religious grouping than as a race which he wanted to be assimilated. A Jewish assembly was chosen by the prefects to decide whether Mosaic law was compatible with civil law and the duties of French citizenship. It met at Paris and was then theatrically reconstituted as a Great Sanhedrin. This Sanhedrin, composed like its predecessor in Jerusalem of forty-five rabbis and twenty-six laymen, met in February 1807 and received considerable publicity.

Napoleon, on campaign in Poland and East Prussia, issued orders to the assembly (Great Sanhedrin). Its major task was to distinguish between unchangeable religious aspects of the laws of Moses and the changeable political features. In addition it was to arrange that at least one third of all Jewish marriages should be mixed, organize the Jewish religion, establish conditions under which Jews could engage in commerce, and forbid Jews to escape the draft by hiring substitutes.

The Great Sanhedrin, which dissolved itself after a month, did not accomplish all that Napoleon desired. It did agree to no more than one consistorial synagogue per department and a central consistory at Paris. It also agreed to civil marriage and the abolition of polygamy, such economic measures as seemed necessary, and military service without substitution. This last measure was markedly effective in promoting assimilation of the Jews, for they were no longer to be a group apart, but would serve alongside the Christians. The assembly refused to make arrangements to repress usury and to regulate the practice of certain professions by the Jews, but it did ask the government to hasten the "social reform of the Jews."

A decree for this purpose, and concentrating on the repression of usury, was appended to a government document published on March 17, 1808, to regulate Jewish religious practices. The regulations contained arrangements similar to those in the Organic Articles. The Jews for religious purposes were grouped into territorial circumscriptions, in each of which a consistory of laymen would be in charge. Rabbis were not to be paid by the state.

The decree on business practices annulled the debts of minors, women, and soldiers, forced Jewish creditors to prove they had furnished capital unless the debtor was a merchant, and authorized the courts to reduce or suppress interest in arrears and to offer a delay in payment. It was actually applied only in Alsace-Lorraine and the Rhineland, and meant that debts owed to Jews there simply were not paid. But the number of complaints against Jewish usury did decline.

Another decree, of July 20, 1808, again designed to eliminate differentiation of the Jews, forced them publicly to declare a surname. Unfortunately for assimilation, many Jews chose surnames that distinguished them from the rest of the population.

But the Napoleonic legislation did hasten the assimilation of the Jews. It removed all excuse for popular uprisings against them. The government took an audacious step across a new frontier when, with the exception of religious expenses, it placed the Jewish religion on the same plane as the Catholic or Protestant. This action did more to effect the assimilation of the Jews in France than any of Napoleon's other measures.[3]

Contemporaries thought that Napoleon's policy favored the Jews, and Jewish communities throughout Europe applauded his efforts. In the Papal States the Jews were allowed to leave the ghetto. Though the Jews in Holland had been declared citizens in 1796, the special tax on them was eliminated only in 1809. In Bavaria the Jews did not become citizens, but in 1813 they obtained freedom of worship. In Württemberg Jews could own land and practice a trade. Baden extended religious tolerance to them in 1808.

The Duchy of Warsaw was the one place where Napoleon had to backtrack on his Jewish policy. Its constitution at first granted Jews the same rights as Christians. This caused such an outcry that in 1809 the Jews lost their political rights for ten years

[3] On St. Helena Napoleon said that he had encouraged the Jews because he wanted them to give up usury, so he could look upon all of his subjects as brothers.

except in the cases of individuals who paid for a political license. Later they needed authorization to marry. In 1808 they were forbidden to buy land without authorization, and in 1812 to farm state land. In the same year the Jewish community received the right to pay a tribute in place of military service.

Freemasonry under the Consulate and Empire was a kind of deist religion succeeding to some of the cults of the Revolutionary decade. The Grand Orient, the grand lodge of the Masons in France, was interested above all in maintaining unity in the face of the Catholic renaissance; it succeeded in doing so by permitting a variety of rites. The Grand Orient never flourished so well in France as under the Empire; it increased its strength from approximately three hundred lodges in 1800 to 886 lodges and 337 chapters in 1814. It even had twelve lodges in Warsaw in 1810. Napoleon did not object to its success. Near the end of his life he stated that he had encouraged the Freemasons "a little" because they fought the Pope.

Napoleon's religious policy, whether considered Revolutionary or reactionary, was "enlightened." He favored the Freemasons, whose outlook was rational and who had flourished especially in the 18th century. Earlier enlightened despots had attempted, without wholly succeeding, to put Jews on the same footing as their other subjects. Like them, Napoleon was tolerant of diverse religions. Above all, he resumed the policy of the early Revolutionaries of subjecting the Roman Catholic Church to the state by controlling appointments and by making it financially dependent on the government. From the historian's point of view, however, the Catholic Church and the Papacy were the chief beneficiaries.

·VII·

THE EDUCATOR

Education in France today is distinguished from that in other major western democracies by its centralized control. Such centralization springs from the existence of an influential teaching corporation (a body with special legal status) which was the creation of Napoleon. Changes since his time have tended to be within the framework of his University, the name given to this teaching body. The *lycée*, the second most important education institution established by Napoleon, still exists, still a school for the elite as it was in Napoleon's day, when he expected it to produce army officers and government officials.

In the decade before Bonaparte came to power numerous proposals (most of which stayed on paper) revealed the Revolutionaries' ideas on education. The Revolutionaries, under the influence of the 18th-century philosophes, considered education to be a function of the state; this was a new concept at the end of the 18th century. The best-known Revolutionary project was drawn up by the famous philosophe, Marie-Jean de Condorcet.

Both the National Assembly (September 3, 1791) and the Convention decreed the organization of "Public Instruction common to all citizens, that part which is indispensable to all men being free." The Convention added, on September 15, 1793, that instruction would be divided into three progressive ranks of primary, secondary, and higher education. This was the first time such a principle had been introduced. Secondary education would be adapted to the technical as well as cultural needs of society, and higher education should take more account of scientific progress. French language, literature, and history were to be at least as important as classical culture.

The similarities between the plan adopted by the Convention and the actions of Napoleon show that he based his educational program on that of the Revolution. Both envisaged a national, all-encompassing system in which elementary education would be practical in nature; both were designed to promote nationalism and patriotism; and both called for strict governmental control.

The Constitution of the Year III laid down the basic principles of such a national system of education: the national government would pay for the lodging of primary-school teachers; there was to be at least one secondary school for every two departments; a National Institute was given the responsibility for "collecting discoveries and perfecting the arts and sciences." The individual institutions of public instruction were not to have any official relations with one another; the only bond among them was to be over-all control by the Minister of the Interior. Citizens were guaranteed the right to found private establishments for education and instruction. National festivals to foster feelings of fraternity and patriotism, and to enhance respect for the Constitution and laws, were deemed a part of the educational process. Starting with the Year XII young men would not be enrolled as voters unless they were literate and could carry on a mechanical occupation.

The education principles of the Constitution were applied in a law of 3 Brumaire, Year IV (October 25, 1795), which remained the academic charter of France until 1802. Secularization of education was implied in this law.

The Revolutionary governments were too busy with other matters to focus the necessary attention on education. Schools were hampered by a lack of both books and personnel. Public primary education sank to a level lower than that of 1789.

The status of secondary education was somewhat better because the Revolutionaries had established about a hundred central schools, so named because they were placed at the center of the primary schools of each department. They were supposed to inspire devotion to the ideals of the Revolution. The only state boarding school was the former College of Louis the Great (in France colleges are secondary schools), renamed College Equality, to which thirty other colleges were united. Under the Directory it received the name Prytanée français; there the "pupils of the country," star students educated at the expense of the government, were maintained.

Only higher education, which was not separated from secondary schooling by a hard and fast line, profited from the changes made during the Revolution. The Convention had created special schools, independent of one another: the Museum of Natural History, the Polytechnic School, the Course of Modern Oriental Languages at the Bibliothèque nationale. There were also schools of medicine at Paris, Montpellier, and Strasbourg. The Ministry of the Interior had control of several establishments of higher education; among these were the universities of Turin and Genoa (the only ones not isolated from one another), three pharmacy schools, the Observatory, the School of Painting, Sculpture and Architecture, and the Collège de France. The Lycée de Paris and the Lycée des Arts were private institutions of higher education. The degree of institutional independence reflected the decentralization of the Revolutionary periods. Topping the whole structure was the Institute. Its 144 members were divided into the three classes of Physical and Mathematical Sciences, Moral and Political Sciences, and Literature and Fine Arts.

By the time Bonaparte came to power, freedom of teaching,

which had benefited only the monarchists and the Catholics, had been limited by decrees of 27 Brumaire and 17 Pluviôse, Year VI. These decrees established a surveillance of private schools and barred their pupils from becoming government officials.

Bonaparte shortly discovered that he did not have trained personnel upon whom he could rely to administer his policies. He therefore personally devoted considerable attention to education after his military and diplomatic successes had made him all-powerful within France.

Madame de Staël, the daughter of Jacques Necker and an outstanding literary figure and opponent of Napoleon, declared that Napoleon expected all minds to march before him as though they were soldiers on the drill field—meaning that he wanted education to be used for purposes of indoctrination. In this, too, he was imitating the Revolutionaries, who had stated that "in every primary school . . . the elements of republican morality shall be taught," and "any schoolmaster or schoolmistress who teaches . . . precepts or maxims contrary to republican laws and morality shall be . . . punished." (Republican laws were clear enough; but teachers may have had considerable difficulty in differentiating "republican morality" from other kinds.) Napoleon explained his agreement with this policy: "Young people can hardly avoid accepting whatever version of the facts is presented to them." And again: "So long as people are not taught from infancy whether to be republican or monarchic, Catholic or irreligious, the State will not at all form a nation; it will rest on uncertain and vague bases, it will be constantly exposed to disorder and change."

Napoleon also agreed with the Revolutionaries that "public instruction should be the first object of government." In 1803 Portalis, who headed the state control of religion, wrote, "Public education belongs to the State, for individual families must be directed according to the plan of the great family which includes them all." In conformity with this principle, freedom of instruction was limited far beyond what the Directory had done. Napoleon's attempt to keep the education system secular continued the Revolutionary tradition.

Napoleon expected two things from the schools. First was the training of middle-class boys to be civil and military leaders. For this purpose, secondary education was most important, and, since he was supremely a militarist, Napoleon wanted rigid military discipline in the secondary schools. Secondly, he wanted the educational system to be absolutely uniform. He wanted, he said, to be able to pull his watch out of his pocket at any time and tell what was going on at any school.

Napoleon's aims led, first of all, to a neglect of primary education, which was left in the hands of private individuals, the church, or local authorities, under the supervision of the sub-prefects. Napoleon, in fact, did not want the masses too educated. His whole period in power saw little improvement and little change in elementary education.

A second development stemming from Napoleon's outlook was a neglect of education for girls, for whom he made no provision in his system of public education. He thought the place of the woman was in the home, her task that of pleasing her husband; for this she did not need any formal education. Schools for girls therefore lagged badly during the fourteen-year period of his power.

I don't think it's necessary to occupy ourselves with teaching for girls, they can't be raised better than by their mothers. Public education does not suit them, as they are not called to live in public; manners are everything for them; marriage is their whole destination.[1]

Napoleon distrusted the spirit of free research and criticism he found in higher education. Higher education was therefore to be purely technical or professional, to train youths to perform

[1] Quoted in Jacques Godechot, *Les Institutions de la France sous la Révolution et l'Empire*. Paris: Presses universitaires de la France, 1951, p. 637.

specific tasks; the theoretical and liberal-arts aspects were to be eliminated. Free thinking anywhere was suspect.

Bonaparte at first permitted the Revolutionary system of education to function with only a few minor changes. He liked the Prytanée; on 1 Germinal, Year VIII (March 22, 1800), it became a teaching establishment divided into four sections, one each at Paris, Saint-Germain, Fontainebleau, and Versailles; the last two were shortly afterward moved to Saint-Cyr and Compiègne. At each a hundred free places were set aside for the sons of civilian officials or army officers who had lost their lives in the fulfillment of their duties. On 27 Messidor, Year IX (July 15, 1801), the number of free places was raised to three hundred at Compiègne, which prepared youths especially for the navy and for mechanical arts, and to two hundred at each of the others. When the *lycées* were created, the Prytanée was reduced to the one section at Saint-Cyr, reserved exclusively for sons of soldiers.

There was an Office of Education when Bonaparte came to power; in the Year IX education, fine arts, and the theater were conjoined as a division in the Ministry of the Interior. A more important change was the creation, in 1802, of a Direction of Public Instruction in the Ministry of the Interior and under a Councillor of State; its budget was 5½ million francs for the Year X. A circular showed that Pierre Roederer, appointed to the post on March 12, was expected to inculcate predetermined ideas: "The department of public instruction is a direction of minds by the mind." He was replaced six months later by Antoine Fourcroy.

Far more fundamental than the earlier structural changes was the complete reorganization of primary and secondary education effected by a law of 11 Floréal, Year X (May 1, 1802). The law was the work of Fourcroy, but Bonaparte, looking upon education in large degree as a source of power, took an active part in the deliberations of the Council of State. Receiving the approval of both the Tribunate and the Legislative Body by majorities of 9 to 1, the law put into effect in the field of education the same principle of hierarchical unity which Bonaparte had earlier installed in administration.

Communes were to establish primary schools. The mayors and municipal councils would select the teachers for these schools, on which the subprefects were to report each month to the prefect. The pay scales of elementary teachers were abysmally low. By remaining silent on the matter, the law permitted private schools on the primary level.

Napoleon especially appealed to and relied on the Brothers of the Christian Schools for primary education. Although their order was reconstituted in 1801 when they resumed teaching, the Council of State did not approve their statutes until 1810. The Brothers were extremely popular; Napoleon said the numerous demands for their reinstatement showed their usefulness. Since the Christian Brothers could not staff their schools with their own members, they had to resort to laymen. A good many female teaching congregations, especially for girls schools, were authorized in 1803 and 1804.

There would be three types of secondary education: *lycées* maintained by the national government, private schools, and communal schools. All secondary schools were under the prefects, who, with the subprefects, were to inspect them at least once a year. Municipalities and private citizens might open secondary schools after preliminary authorization by the government. The legal provision that authorization could be revoked each year effectively suppressed freedom of secondary education.

A consular decree of 19 Vendémiaire, Year XII (October 10, 1803), called for an "Administrative Bureau" for each communal secondary school. Through this bureau, which included the subprefect and the mayor, the government intervened in the appointment of teachers: the bureau was to recommend two candidates, of whom the Minister of the Interior appointed one. Another decree of the same day provided that private secondary schools were to have at least three teachers and fifty students, and follow the mode of teaching prescribed for the communal secondary schools. Authorization was necessary for existing schools as well as for those to be created.

Napoleon also permitted church-sponsored "little seminaries" on the secondary level. In theory they were to train future priests; in actuality, thousands attended with no thought of entering the priesthood.

The main purpose of the law of 1802 (Year X) was to create the *lycée,* which would supplant the central schools and be more consonant with Bonaparte's desires. He considered the central schools suspect as strongholds of Jacobinism and free thought; besides, the *bourgeoisie* avoided them since they offered no religious instruction. They were far more decentralized than he liked.

Each area served by a court of appeal was to have at least one *lycée.* Napoleon had foreseen forty-five, but only thirty-seven existed in 1808. Eventually forty-five were established, four of them at Paris. Each *lycée* had a headmaster and an administrative council appointed by Bonaparte. The First Consul was to appoint three inspectors-general who would visit at least once a year each *lycée* except those of Paris. Bonaparte selected all the faculty members from lists of two or three nominees for each position. The *lycée* teachers were materially better off than those of the central schools had been.

The government gave practical endorsement to the *lycées.* Scholarships of 700 francs each were provided for 6,400 students, school sites were donated, and the schoolmasters who had the most pupils admitted to *lycées* were rewarded. Of the scholarships, 2,400 were to go to sons of soldiers and officials and 4,000 to secondary school pupils who had survived an examination and competition. (The scholarships went begging; only 3,000 were actually awarded.) Nonscholarship holders could be either boarding pupils or day students.

The *lycées* were to teach classical languages, rhetoric, logic, morality, and the elements of the mathematical and physical sciences. Until 1809 each *lycée* had a literary section with Latin as the base and a science section based on mathematics. Instruction was actually less modern than intended because literature was stressed more than science and the initial curriculum did not provide for either philosophy or modern languages.

The government, acting through the Minister of the Interior, closely regulated what subjects might be taught. History was not initially taught as a separate subject because the authorities considered it dangerous. Roederer told the Legislative Body when it was considering the school reorganization of 1802 that history should be combined with geography and public economy, rather than becoming a separate subject, because people can learn history themselves by reading it attentively. A later decree, issued on 19 Frimaire, Year XI, provided that history would be taught in the last three classes of the Latin section—first the elements of chronology and of ancient history, then history to the founding of the French Empire, and finally the history of France. Much the same regimen applied to geography. Napoleon was probably responsible for having even this much history in the schools.[2]

A decision of September 19, 1809, stated that the *lycée* course of studies would no longer be divided into Latin and mathematics sections. *Lycée* pupils would now all receive the same instruction: two years of grammar, two of humanities, one year of rhetoric, and one of special mathematics. Each *lycée* was to have nine teachers, plus a tenth for those *lycées* in departmental capitals. Philosophy was to be taught in the humanities and was aimed at combating the materialist tendencies of the 18th century.

[2] In 1807 Napoleon decided that the Collège de France would have three chairs of history: Critical Literary History, Military History of France, and History of Legislation in France.

The government decided what books might be used. The decree of 19 Frimaire, Year XI (December 9, 1802), called for a library of 1,500 volumes in each *lycée,* all the *lycées* to have the same books. The police made sure there were no competing texts. Some of the texts adopted were commissioned by the government; others were adopted merely because they were safe. As Napoleon told his Minister of the Interior when instructing him to have a continuation of the history of France written, "When this work . . . has appeared, no one will have the will and the patience to do another, especially when, far from being encouraged by the police, he will be discouraged by it." Books the government did not inspire were judged according to their attitude on absolute power. A censor appointed by Napoleon was to examine all books and illustrations entering the *lycées* and prohibit those deemed dangerous.

In 1809 the baccalaureate examination, the notorious "bac" for which French students today cram and sometimes cheat, was instituted. It covered everything taught in the upper classes of the *lycées,* and passing it was a prerequisite for the baccalaureate degree and hence for admission to higher education. During the first year thirty-one students received the degree; in 1813, it was awarded to 1,700.

Napoleon also devoted considerable attention to technical education of all kinds, including reorganization of the Polytechnic School. In 1808 the last remaining section of the Prytanée, at Saint-Cyr, was replaced by the special military school founded in 1802 that became a famous military academy for the training of cavalry and infantry officers. Other technical schools founded by Napoleon included those already mentioned in the chapter on economic development.

The law of 11 Floréal, Year X, also looked to the creation of quite a large number of special schools. On the professional level there were eventually seven medical faculties. The need for schools of law was particularly great, but Napoleon created no new ones. The twelve law faculties organized by the law of 22 Ventôse, Year XII (March 11, 1804), and the decree of the fourth complementary day of the same year were merely existing law schools with a new name and organization. Bonaparte was to name five inspectors-general and to choose each teacher or substitute from two names, one submitted by the teachers and one by the inspectors-general. Distrusting the teaching of law because it touched the great economic, legislative, and social problems of the day, Napoleon restricted it to narrow technicalities.

In assessing, from Napoleon's point of view, the reorganization of public education, we must keep the *lycée* particularly in mind. It was the central point of his thinking—and it was a failure.

In 1806 there were 370 communal and 377 private secondary schools enrolling 50,000 pupils, as contrasted with 15,000 pupils in the *lycées*. Most municipalities without a *lycée* changed the name of their central schools to secondary schools. In addition, there were 4,500 private schools, above the level of primary schools but not strong enough to be secondary schools, which had about 25,000 pupils. The law of 1802 had failed, for the *lycées* could not withstand the competition of the private and communal schools.

The *lycées* did not prove more popular for a number of reasons. The *bourgeoisie* did not send their sons to them because these schools were looked upon as being irreligious and as being barracks to form soldiers. There could be no questioning the military discipline of the *lycées*, where military exercises were required of all pupils. The government regulated them very closely, even controlling the games of the students. Yet there were also religious exercises; the government, hoping to forestall the students' falling under the influence of fanatical or royalist priests, named a chaplain for each *lycée*. There was, moreover,

THE ORGANIZATION OF THE IMPERIAL UNIVERSITY

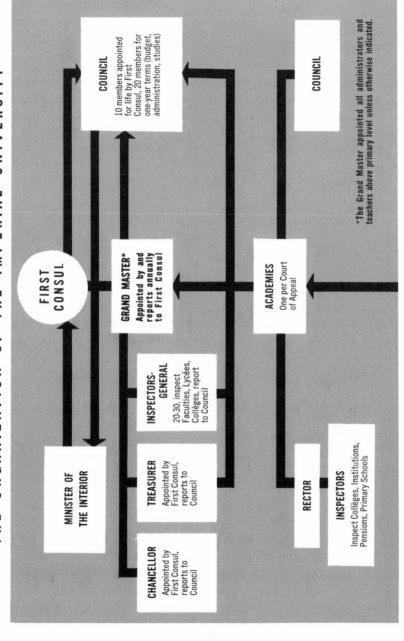

FIRST CONSUL

COUNCIL
10 members appointed for life by First Consul, 20 members for one-year terms (budget, administration, studies)

COUNCIL

GRAND MASTER*
Appointed by and reports annually to First Consul

ACADEMIES
One per Court of Appeal

MINISTER OF THE INTERIOR

INSPECTORS-GENERAL
20-30, inspect Faculties, Lycées, Collèges, report to Council

CHANCELLOR
Appointed by First Consul, reports to Council

TREASURER
Appointed by First Consul, reports to Council

RECTOR

INSPECTORS
Inspect Collèges, Institutions, Pensions, Primary Schools

*The Grand Master appointed all administrators and teachers above primary level unless otherwise indicated.

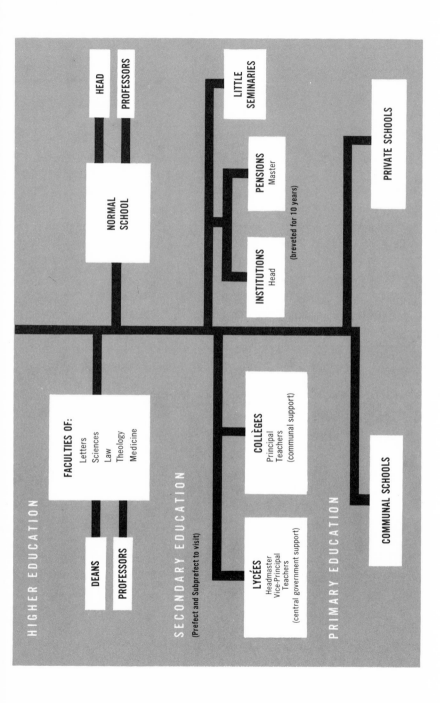

a monastic type of discipline. For example, the students could not leave the school grounds without permission, and during meals they were read to and had to maintain complete silence.

Fourcroy foresaw a budget of 7,310,000 francs for all public instruction under the law of 1802, 2 million francs more than before. Napoleon would have liked the *lycées* to cost the government almost nothing, but their cost rose from 418,000 francs in Year XI to 2,921,000 francs in the Year XIII. The actual amount spent on education over this three-year period, however, represented a saving of 1,725,000 francs, as the central schools—charged to the departmental budgets—had been more expensive. To reduce expenses further, Napoleon ordered a reduction in the number of teachers and administrators, and on 10 Germinal, Year XIII (March 30, 1805), said that some of the 3,000 national students should pay half their fees and some pay 140 francs, though some free places would still be retained. A decree of 3 Floréal (April 22) of the same year said that each *lycée* should have 150 students supported by the government—20 of them completely, 50 at three fourths, and 80 on a half scholarship.

Napoleon's second major contribution to education, more important even than the *lycée* and its accompaniments, was the establishment of the Imperial University. This was a state teaching monopoly, created by a law of 1806 and a decree of 1808. Not a university as we use the term, it encompassed all levels and types of instruction.

Napoleon had two main reasons for creating the University. One was to give the *lycées* the pupils they lacked. The other was to get a body of properly trained and—especially—properly oriented teachers. Only then could education have the desired indoctrination effect. In Napoleon's words, "There never will be a fixed political state of things in this country until we have a corps of teachers instructed in established principles." He further said that his principal goal in the establishment of a teaching body was to "have a means of directing political and moral opinion."

The University monopoly did not constitute a sudden, radical departure from earlier developments in the field of education. It was only an application of the principle of complete state control in favor even during the Revolution, a perfecting of existing academic institutions. What Napoleon did was tie together more firmly the different parts of the instructional structure established by the law of 1802, establish an official hierarchy, and appoint a head with extensive powers.

Napoleon had been mulling over the idea of the University for some time before putting it into effect. The first trace of the project appeared in 1804 at the end of the Consulate. In a note of 27 Pluviôse, Year XIII (February 15, 1805), Napoleon formulated for the first time his idea of a university body. The victory at Austerlitz and the ensuing Treaty of Pressburg finally gave him enough sway over public opinion to dare to go ahead.

The Council of State under Napoleon's presidency considered nine drafts of proposals for a teaching body. It was evident that the views of the Council did not agree with those of Napoleon; the very word *university* had been made so odious by its religious ties and monopolistic tendencies during the *ancien régime* that the Revolution had outlawed it. Jean Portalis opposed the idea of a teaching monopoly on the grounds that it would deprive fathers of the right to say where their children should go to school. Louis Fontanes agreed wholeheartedly with Napoleon's idea:

> On the morrow of a revolution, upon coming out of anarchy and in the presence of hostile parties, unity of views and of government are necessary in education as in all things. France needs, for a time at least, a single University, and the University a single head.[3]

A law of May 10, 1806, scheduled to become effective in 1810, provided for the formation of a special teaching body in order to offer a uniform and complete education. This teaching body was the Imperial University, established by decree on March 17,

---

[3] Quoted in A. Aulard, *Napoleon Ier et le monopole universitaire.* Paris: Armand Colin, 1911, p. 163.

1808. The decree, which organized in detail the various parts of the University, also laid down the bases of teaching. Among them were fidelity to the Emperor, the imperial monarchy, and the Napoleonic dynasty. The most surprising basis was the doctrine of the Catholic religion, which obviously contradicted the spirit of the Revolution. (The decree originally read "Christian religion," but it was changed to "Catholic religion.") The Council of State in March of 1810 said the University was to inspire love of government and the fourth dynasty, and a horror of theories subversive of the social order.

Both the law and the decree implemented the principle of centralization. The law stated:

> No school, no educational institution whatsoever, can be formed outside the Imperial University and without the authorization of its head. No one may open a school or teach publicly without being a member of the Imperial University and graduated from one of its Faculties.[4]

The decree left no doubt that Napoleon's would be the final voice:

> We reserve to ourselves . . . to amend . . . every decision, regulation or act emanating from the council of the University or the grandmaster, whenever we shall deem it useful for the good of the State.

The teaching hierarchy was divided into primary, secondary, and higher orders, as had been decreed during the Revolution. For the first time the national government regulated primary schools.

The head of the University, with the title of Grand Master, was Louis de Fontanes, selected because he came from a family which had both Catholic and Protestant members and because he was a famous literary figure whom Napoleon was pleased to have rally to him. As Grand Master, Fontanes was not a functionary of the Minister of the Interior, but had extensive independent powers. He made all appointments and promotions,

---

[4] *Ibid.*, p. 170.

granted all diplomas, proposed regulations on teaching, administration, and discipline, and rendered a financial accounting. Under the Grand Master there were a chancellor, who was keeper of the archives and the seal, a special University treasurer, and twenty to thirty inspectors-general.

There was also a Council of the University, a body often advocated during the Revolution. It had ten members chosen by Napoleon for life—six inspectors and four rectors—and twenty chosen for a year by education officials from among headmasters of the *lycées,* deans and professors of the faculties, and the inspectors. The Council had important powers. It decreed the budgets; heard reports of the inspectors-general; and judged all questions relative to the policing, accountability, and general administration of the schools. It drew up and proclaimed the decrees that formed the code which continued to govern the University even after Napoleon's day, under the restored Bourbons (1814–30) and the Orleanist Louis Philippe (1830–48).

For purposes of administering public instruction, the Empire was divided into twenty-six areas, one for each court of appeal, known as academies. Each academy was under a rector aided by one or more inspectors and a council. The rector was chosen for five years by the Grand Master and could be reappointed. Under his orders, one or two inspectors, recommended by him and named by the Grand Master, were to visit the schools. The Grand Master also named the Academic Council of ten members.

The secondary schools other than the *lycées* had to bear special imposts and other burdens. The teachers in the *collèges*—the name given to the communal secondary schools at the time the University monopoly was created—were forced into celibate living in a kind of monastic community; *lycée* teachers might marry. Until 1808 private schools were supposed to turn over to the University 5 per cent of their student fees, but it seems that the assessment was not paid regularly. After 1808 the fiscal contribution amounted to 5 per cent of the cost of a full boarding student for each student, regardless of whether he fell into this category. In addition, heads of secondary schools had to make payments to the government ranging from 50 to 100 francs a year. Teachers offering a higher course in sciences or letters paid 50 francs a year; those offering a higher course in law or medicine paid double that amount. It was these fiscal requirements which particularly galled and damaged private schools.

The *collèges* differed from the *lycées* only in degree, not in kind; they even had the same disciplinary regime. The *collèges* were divided into two classes, based on whether they offered instruction in addition to the humanities. Even some important cities had to content themselves with this kind of school, of which there were five hundred at the end of the Empire. The *collèges* had neither the prestige nor the governmental backing enjoyed by the *lycées*.

Two categories of higher education institutions were permitted to remain outside the University. The first was composed of those founded during the Revolution. The other was the seminaries. Neither of these had to be approved by the head of the University.

Napoleon had taken several measures to placate the Catholics, but he did not entirely succeed. He had included religion as a basis of teaching; the Grand Master, the Council, and the inspectors took the religious bases of instruction very seriously.

Yet some of the clergy were not satisfied. They realized that the substitution of the *lycées* for the central schools was not a victory for Catholicism. It was, in the eyes of contemporaries, merely a simplification and an improvement of the former schools, an adaptation of the new teaching to the current needs, customs, and prejudices. Theology teachers had to conform to the dispositions of the Declaration of Gallican Liberties. Many of the Catholic institutions lost their rating as secondary schools. Napoleon aimed to suppress the little seminaries by a decree of April 9, 1809. There had been complaints about their competition and the denigrating of government institutions by the priests. The clause relevant to the little seminaries stated that all schools except seminaries, which students could enter only if they had a bachelor's degree from a faculty of letters, would be administered by the University and be subject to its rules. The little seminaries, whose students did not have the requisite degrees, thus fell under state control. But at the same time Napoleon authorized departments, cities, bishops, or private citizens to establish secondary schools for children destined for the church.

In the field of higher education, the decree of March 17, 1808, created ten faculties of Catholic theology, one for each archdiocese. The aim was to replace the relatively independent seminaries with teaching strictly controlled by the state—favor was extended, but at the price of surveillance. Each faculty was to have chairs of church history, dogma, and evangelical morality, but it could have more if the number of pupils so required. The decree also provided for two Protestant faculties. The one at Geneva had five chairs; the one to be at Strasbourg did not materialize.

The chief innovation in higher education was the replacement of the old faculties of arts with two faculties—of letters and of sciences. They were to dispense both general culture and degrees, rather than to prepare students for a particular career or profession. The degrees they granted were the baccalaureate, licentiate, and doctorate. This conferring of degrees following passage of an examination became their main function, especially for the faculties of letters; teaching was only ancillary.

There was to be one of each kind of faculty at each *lycée* in the chief town of each academy; the faculties were, in fact, only prolongations of the *lycées*. The Science Faculty was to have at least four chairs: two in mathematics, one of natural history, and one for chemistry and physics. The faculties of letters were each to have at least three men, and to teach literature, philosophy, and history. In several places the rector of the academy was the

157

dean of the faculty, for reasons of economy and because this prevented the faculties from developing autonomy and a sense of independence. There were fifteen sciences faculties and twenty-seven letters faculties; the former were permitted wide horizons, but a narrow and antiquated program was imposed on the faculties of letters. History teaching occupied a very small place, being limited to principles of chronology, the great historical epochs, and the concordance of ancient and modern geography.

The teaching at Paris was more highly developed. The Faculty of Sciences, for example, was to have eight instructors, two from the *lycées,* and two each from the Collège de France, the Museum of Natural History, and the Polytechnic School. The Paris faculties had by far the best students, the pupils of the normal school.

The normal school at Paris was provided for by the decree of March 17, 1808, which stated that the normal boarding school would train three hundred students a year to be teachers. For reasons of economy it had only fifteen pupils in sciences and fifty-eight in letters in 1812. The discipline, contrary to law, was almost the same as in the *lycées.* The pupils, state-supported and exempt from military service, had to agree to serve the state for ten years after graduation. A critical spirit persisted at this school after it had vanished from almost every other one.[5] No serious attempt was made to form normal classes in the *lycées* and *collèges* as the decree had promised.

In February 1813 the law faculties had the largest enrollment, 4,034 students. Medicine had less than half as many, 1,929. Then followed letters with 1,841, theology with 596, and sciences with 459 students.

The University's most prized privilege was naturally its theoretical teaching monopoly. In addition, it had the right to its own

[5] The normal school faculty did not express a spirit of Bonapartism. François Guizot, for example, made clear allusions in his history lectures to Napoleon's despotism and conquering ambitions.

budget, free of any semblance of control by the Legislative Body. This was contrary to the practices of accountability established by the Revolution. The initial expenses of establishing the University were met by a one-year million-franc loan at 5 per cent interest from the sinking fund. Napoleon wanted the University to be as nearly self-supporting as possible. Among the sources of its income were the payments for the granting of degrees and certificates (the medical and law faculties kept 90 per cent of their fees, hence a certain fiscal autonomy). The University's 5 per cent tribute for secondary pupils, described above, brought in an average of more than 1.75 million francs a year from 1809 through 1813. Budgeted University receipts totaled about 2,600,000 francs a year, but the University needed additional funds from the government; budgeted University expenses in 1812, for example, totaled 3,862,578 francs. In addition to the sums spent on the University, the Ministry of the Interior in 1812 spent 3,142,250 francs for public instruction on establishments of higher education, such as the Polytechnic School, which were not a part of the University.

The monopoly of the University was largely a façade. In part this situation resulted from the unpopularity of the government schools, in part from the double-crossing of Napoleon by Fontanes, who did everything possible to encourage ecclesiastical schools. The monopoly was initially only a more regulated supervision of teaching obtained through a legal fiction introducing all private schools into the University framework. The private schools still furnished as much competition to the *lycées* and communal colleges as under the law of 1802, for they were fortified by the prestige of the University and guaranteed against government arbitrariness by Fontanes and by the very word *University*. Forced to act by lack of teaching personnel and lack of funds, Napoleon had to permit private and church schools to reopen, but the government supposedly regulated them strictly. Although the Christian Brothers were theoretically under the

University, their dependence was purely nominal. They did not have to take the regular oath, were exempted from military service, and were favored in other ways.

Napoleon was determined, however, to make the University monopoly a reality; so the Council of State declared in 1810 that there should be as few private schools as possible. Napoleon's last important step in this direction was a decree of November 15, 1811. Admittedly he was influenced by statistics showing that in 1809, 1810, and 1811 there were almost as many students in private schools as in the *lycées* and *collèges* combined.

On the secondary level there could now be only one ecclesiastical school per department, and it had to follow the curriculum of the *lycée* or *collège*. All teachers had to be members of the University. The bishops could nominate seminary directors and teachers, but Napoleon—or the government—would do the actual appointing. The government further supervised, in accordance with the Organic Articles, the doctrines taught in the seminaries, to make sure they conformed to the Gallican Liberties.

All the day pupils of private schools were to attend the *lycée* or *collège* if there was one in the town; the private institutions could accept boarding students only after the *lycées* were full.[6] In cities without a *lycée* or *collège*, the private schools were not to teach on a level higher than the humanities (*i.e.*, the first four classes of the *lycée*), and the boarding schools not above grammar and elementary arithmetic and geometry (equivalent to the first two classes of the *lycée*). All schools were to be governed by the University. The prefects were again to supervise every educational establishment.

But the decrees of the "academic blockade" did not bring the results Napoleon expected even though they resulted in a sub-

[6] In November of 1812, the Council of the University forbade distribution of prizes in private schools located in towns where there were *lycées* or *collèges*.

stantial shift of students to *lycées* and *collèges* from private schools, particularly in 1813. The decrees were not even applied in all of France, and were not stringently enforced even where they were in effect. If they had been enforced, private and ecclesiastical secondary education would virtually have disappeared.

Far from applying the 1811 decree strictly, Fontanes continued to be the accomplice of private instruction. He favored clericals, and indirectly favored opposition to the Empire; he flattered Napoleon publicly while having pupils make declamations against the Emperor, after Napoleon's star had begun to dim in 1813. Yet Fontanes kept his functions until February 17, 1815, when the position of Grand Master was replaced with a powerless Presidency of the Council.

In the territories under his control, Napoleon's educational activity varied greatly. The areas most influenced were the Duchy of Warsaw (where the French completely revised the system of government control of education) and Italy. In Naples Murat decreed a system as similar to that of France as circumstances permitted. And in the Kingdom of Italy, Napoleon personally took the initiative in creating a system of public education which he expected to contribute to the moral unification of the country. Other areas received *lycées* and *collèges*, and sometimes even, as in the Illyrian provinces, a general regulation of public instruction.

Much of Napoleon's attention to education was dictated by propagandistic motives. Yet he looked upon schools as more than a source of power; he was also aiming for a system of education which would so shape French youth that they would be reasonable and reasoning people. Although the *lycées* placed less stress than the central schools on science, science had a more important place in the schools than before 1795. Taking up the work of intellectual emancipation undertaken by the philosophes and Revolutionaries, he prevented the Catholic Church from becoming once again master of national teaching. Even if the ideas of the Revolution were deformed in the University, they were still present.

Hampered by a lack of resources (the reason why he waited until 1811 to issue his decree requiring all teachers to belong to the University), Napoleon was unable to erect the kind of educational structure he wanted. His dream of directing the intellectual formation of the youth remained far from fulfilled.

But his work in the field of education cannot be accounted a complete failure from his viewpoint. He achieved his immediate goal of having the schools prepare and train functionaries for the government. Though accepting part of the Revolutionary tradition and building on the Revolutionary institutions, he put his own imprint on the educational system of France. The University monopoly on public education and teaching lasted until 1850. Under the Third Republic (1870–1940), there was repeated agitation for re-establishment of the monopoly, a step which would have removed the church from educational activities. Though the monopoly has not been restored, the University of France, a much enlarged version of the one founded by Napoleon, still exists, and it still controls all types of educational activities. With its rigid hierarchical organization, the University remains a characteristic and durable Napoleonic creation.

An interesting and important result of this centralization has been a decline in French contributions to educational philosophy; the centralization and systematization tend to prevent personal initiative. Yet the hierarchy from classroom teacher to Minister of Education has given the French educational system stability and continuity, and the centralization has made the classroom teachers independent of local political and religious pressures.

·VIII·

THE PROPAGANDIST

Prior to the French Revolution, public opinion was of relatively minor interest to rulers of continental European countries. Even in England, where Parliament had been supreme since the Glorious Revolution of 1688, the voters were such a small percentage that they could hardly be said to represent a real public opinion. But the French Revolution brought, and Napoleon continued at least in theory, mass participation in government. It is therefore not surprising to find active propaganda campaigns during both the Revolutionary and the Napoleonic periods. Interested in propaganda as a means of self-aggrandizement as well as for furthering government policy, Napoleon kept the spotlight constantly on himself, performing unerringly in the center ring.

The greatest importance of Napoleon's propaganda is that he was the first to use the machinery of government in a systematic fashion to control public opinion—and that he used it positively to formulate favorable as well as to prevent unfavorable opinion. He was the forerunner of all twentieth-century dictators—none of whom would try to force through a program for which he did not have public support, perhaps gained by a total control of the information available to his subjects. And the value of Napoleon's propaganda, even though it could not compare in refinement or totality with that of today, was well recognized by his opponents.

Although the word *propaganda* has acquired a bad connotation, propaganda itself should not be considered necessarily evil. Its campaigns may be for desirable as well as undesirable purposes, and it should be judged by the type of social response it seeks rather than by the fact that it functions differently from education. It presents only one point of view (which need not be inaccurate) in an attempt to affect in a predetermined manner the attitudes and actions of large groups of people who will not analyze how they reached their point of view. Censorship is necessary if political propaganda is to achieve its purpose.

Propaganda functions best and is most necessary in times of emotional tension. The Napoleonic period was such a time, for France had but fourteen months of peace during the whole period. The changing status of the war profoundly affected Napoleon's propaganda activities. An understanding of these activities should be based on a consideration of what he tried to persuade the public to believe; of the media of communications, government spokesmen, and propagandist devices involved in reaching the people; and of the probable results.

Napoleon's message, less subtly stated than is true of modern propaganda, included castigation of the enemy (of Great Britain, his most persistent opponent, he said, "It is too bad Hell is not at England's disposal; she would vomit it over the whole universe"); a bolstering of the morale of his side and an attempt to weaken that of his opponents; depiction of a string of French victories won at low cost; and a portrayal of the infallibility of the French government and what it accomplished for the people. Napoleon tried to suppress disagreeable news: "Whenever news arrives which is disagreeable to the government, its publication must be delayed until people are so sure of the truth that it no longer needs to be said because everybody knows it." The *Moniteur,* the official paper of the government, did not mention the battle of Trafalgar at all; other papers did so only after a delay of two months, and then as news coming from Britain so as to soften the effect. Napoleon berated the enemy for the very type of news-doctoring in which he himself indulged.

The newspaper was an even more powerful molder of public opinion then than it is today, and Napoleon relied more upon newspapers than on any other medium to put across his message. Ranking first in his journalistic lists was the *Moniteur.* All the provincial papers had to rely primarily on it for their items of information or interpretation. Although the *Moniteur* remained private property, various government officials wrote its articles. The Minister of Police wrote most of the domestic articles. He was aided by the Minister of the Interior for the articles under the title "Interior" and members of Napoleon's office staff for the material under "Paris." "Miscellany" presented an opportunity for various officials to include domestic propaganda articles. The materials on the Institute, Poetry, Literature, and the Theater were likewise official. The Minister of Foreign Affairs took care of most of the releases on foreign and diplomatic matters and inserted more articles than any other official.

For religious news Napoleon in 1806 established a *Journal des Curés* to replace all other religious papers, which he had suppressed. In order to reach the Italian-speaking population under his control, he subsidized and fostered an Italian newspaper published in Paris, *Il Corriere d'Italia.* And so it went: in every area under his authority there was an official or semiofficial newspaper to present the Napoleonic point of view.

He said he would judge papers not "on the evil they have done, but on the little good they have done." He must also, however, have judged them by their evil, actual or potential, for he took action against them almost as soon as he assumed power. A decree of 27 Nivôse, Year VIII (January 17, 1800), stated: "All papers which insert articles contrary to the respect due the social pact, to the sovereignty of the people, to the glory of the armies, or who publish invectives against friendly or allied governments . . . will be suppressed immediately." It was this decree which permitted reduction of the number of Paris newspapers from seventy-three to thirteen, so that he could more easily give them the supervision they so obviously, to his way of thinking, needed. By 1811 the number of Parisian papers had dropped to four, the others having gone bankrupt or having been suppressed by the government. The Directory had also taken violent measures against the press, but Bonaparte surpassed it by forbidding establishment of new papers; once a paper was suppressed, its editors could not hope to publish under a different title.

Fear of the press must have played a role in Napoleon's limiting the number of provincial papers in 1807 to one per department, each supervised by the prefect of that department. The provincial press prior to then had not undergone the same censorship as had the Paris press. On November 6, 1807, Joseph Fouché as Minister of Police forbade the provincial press to print any article on politics which it did not excerpt from the *Moniteur,* under penalty of suppression; three years later a decree reiterated this policy. The police might suppress a paper, or a prefect in the provinces might take action.

Napoleon suppressed papers in subject territories as well as in France. In 1811 a decree stated that any paper in the Confederation of the Rhine which published political news not extracted from the *Moniteur* would be suppressed. In non-French territory it was the Foreign Minister, working through his resident agents, who was given responsibility for suppressing inimical papers, or a satellite ruler might act. Some papers were suspended temporarily for infractions of Napoleon's will.

Another negative means of controlling public opinion was censorship. In Napoleonic France there was censorship of letters, of the press (including pamphlets), and of books. Letters were censored by the post office. Pamphlets were regularly reported on by the prefect of police in Paris and the Ministry of Police, and prefects reported on both critical and friendly pamphlets published in their departments. The Ministry of Police had charge of censoring the press. There was a regular routine for daily censorship of newspapers, with a Press Bureau in the Ministry charged with their supervision.

The censorship concerned itself primarily with the political part of the paper; that fact explains why only political items were mentioned in the 1807 decree on provincial press excerpts. Certain topics remained completely taboo; others were merely on the forbidden list for a period of time or had to be discussed in the *Moniteur* before being taken up elsewhere. Among the forbidden topics were criticism of religion, the laws or morals, and anything reminiscent of political faction. The rigid censorship was part of what today would be called a police state.

At first the prefect of police had charge of preliminary censorship of books; by a decree of December 14, 1810, a special censorship bureau known as the General Direction of Printing and Bookselling was created in the Ministry of the Interior to handle this censorship. Submission of a book manuscript prior to publication was, however, voluntary rather than compulsory. Publication was forbidden if the book was held to be contrary to the interests of peace, the state, public order, or the Christian religion; the Director-General could order changes in the manuscript to make it acceptable for publication. Even though a book had been approved by the censorship, it might later be seized if the government considered it dangerous. Authors of unfriendly books were subject to arbitrary arrest.

Napoleon's instructions, moreover, were sometimes confusing, as in his message to Eugène de Beauharnais, viceroy in the Kingdom of Italy: "I want you to suppress completely the censorship of books. This country already has a narrow enough mind without straitening it any more. Of course the publication of any work contrary to the government would be stopped."

In accordance with a decree of February 5, 1810, the number

of printers at Paris was limited to sixty, and all printers and book-sellers had to be licensed by the government's censorship bureau. This bureau was also in charge of the distribution of approved books. The Director-General of Printing and Bookselling could order a delay in the printing of a book to allow the imperial censors time to examine the work and propose necessary changes and suppressions.

Newspapers could be controlled in ways other than by censor-ship. For example, the editors had to be approved by the govern-ment—which could also exert control by taxing hostile papers more heavily or even by seizing their property.

The preceding measures were negative and punitive, and earlier governments had resorted to them. It was the positive side of Napoleon's approach to controlling public opinion that was novel, though even here not all of its facets were without precedent. Taken in its totality, however, it did represent a new development in government.

Napoleon used a variety of means to obtain publication of the items he desired. Friendly papers might be well subsidized, in part by guaranteed subscriptions. Nobody today has to be told the importance of government handouts for the newspapers; in a dictatorship they are especially important. Napoleon frequently favored a paper that was in his good graces by granting it exclu-sives or originals on news items. A paper that was forbidden to print official news or could do so only late in the game was seriously handicapped in its fight for survival. As for the *Moni-teur*, Napoleon frequently indicated to his subordinates how many articles they should write and at what intervals. (Among the family rulers, those most important in the propaganda sphere were Joseph and Eugène, and, ranking behind them, Murat.)

Among the temptations Napoleon dangled before the authors whose books were to be part of the glory of his reign were annual pensions and a variety of prizes (some of them never awarded) comparable in our own day to the Stalin or Lenin prizes in the Soviet Union. But these payments did not produce works of the quality Napoleon desired; all the great writers escaped him. Napoleon recognized this fact, but continued to keep artists and writers on his payroll because, as he said, "These fellows are good for nothing under any government. I will, however, give them pensions because, as Head of the State, I ought to do so." He frequently ordered a book on a specific topic—usually historical—and sometimes indicated who was to be its author. In January of 1811 Napoleon ordered the Minister of Police to have the historian Pierre-Édouard Lemontey write a *History of France since the Death of Louis XIV* to contrast the decadence of the Bourbon dynasty with the dynamic Bonapartist era. He encouraged Abbé Halma to continue Valley's *Histoire de France* and the *Abrégé chronologique* of President Hénault, indicating what conclusions were to be reached. Needless to say, the books were to point up Napoleon's successes.

The government's handling of the writing and distribution of pamphlets was more flexible than for any other kind of propaganda material. Almost any official might be called upon to write a pamphlet or to find somebody to do so. Even when Napoleon was not directly responsible for the writing of pamphlets, he took an avid interest in them, but the more confidence he had in a subordinate, the less detailed his instructions were. To boost sales, the price of government pamphlets merely covered the actual costs of printing.

Napoleon looked on handbills and posters as poor media of propaganda, and used them sparingly, generally for material that had first appeared in another form. A good many individuals put proclamations into this form, as a result of either specific or blanket authorization.

In addition to the media already discussed, Napoleon propagandized through rumors, regularly scheduled and special festivals, speeches that might later be published, the theater, music, and the arts.

The festivals featured something for everybody: music, poetry, speeches, *Te Deums,* free theater performances, fireworks, balls, and free food. As time went on, they became more military and less philosophic. Officials other than Napoleon also initiated festivals, which were adapted to the specific area involved. Some took place only in the area concerned—for example, only Italy celebrated Napoleon's coronation as king of Italy—but others were held throughout the empire. Annual festivals celebrated such national holidays as Napoleon's birthday and coronation; irregular festivals celebrated battles, treaties, and such important events in the Bonaparte family as Napoleon's marriage.

Napoleon had subordinates spread rumors to test the state of public opinion, and to help morale and military strategy. In October of 1806, when he was fighting Prussia, Napoleon told Marmont that until the first news arrived, he should spread the rumor that peace had been made. Yet the Emperor was more concerned with the combating of hostile rumors than with planting his own. The police naturally played the most active role in tracking down such rumors, but numerous officials aided in exploding them. Napoleon also used the press to a considerable extent, sometimes canceling a rumor's effectiveness simply by publishing straight news.

Napoleon's treatment of the theater seemed a combination of his policy toward papers and books. Theaters were expected to perform patriotic plays and to glorify Napoleon's name by performing the classics well. Although the number of theaters grew in the first half of his regime, in 1807 he reduced the number in Paris from thirty-three to eight so as to watch them more closely. A Superintendent of Spectacles was in charge of the Théâtre-Français; the other theaters of Paris were each controlled by a prefect of the palace. Napoleon prescribed and proscribed their plays, subsidized them, gave pensions to actors, and ordered a strict preliminary censorship by the Bureau of Theaters under the Division of Public Instruction. In the departments the prefects were charged with the preliminary censorship of plays. Performances might be disallowed even after permission had been received to publish a play because on stage the play would appeal to elements in the population different from its readers. If a play was produced, a police agent, stationed in the audience to make sure that nothing untoward took place, was to analyze it within forty-eight hours of the first performance. After 1806 a new play could be performed only with authorization from the Minister of Police.

Composers were commissioned to write patriotic songs and to write music for the various festivals; some of the outstanding ones were paid regular sums just to adorn the imperial regime. Similarly, painters were paid, foremost among them being the classicist Jacques-Louis David. The government rewarded patriotic poetry and even suggested topics. In 1801 a competition was opened for the best verse on the founding of the Republic; in 1804 the Minister of the Interior rewarded poets and musicians for pieces celebrating Napoleon's coronation. Articles in the *Moniteur* encouraged the use of national subjects and heroes as topics for poems. Architects were commissioned to erect monuments to Napoleon's rule. Especially noteworthy were numerous monuments to the army, including the Arc de Triomphe de l'Étoile. Perhaps the most interesting monuments Napoleon ordered were a big pyramid on the battlefield of Marengo and an elephant made from the melted-down guns of Spanish rebels.

Another art exploited by Napoleon, a lively one, was caricature. Usually he told Fouché what he wanted, and the Minister of Police then relayed his ideas to the artists. One cartoon of late 1806 or early 1807, probably inspired by a French official, showed Napoleon's power flooding the mainland. Alexander I of Russia was clutching a breaking tree on the edge of a cliff, Queen Louise of Prussia was grasping his waist, her husband was clinging to her while supporting a half-drowned Elector of Hesse. In the background John Bull was tossing in a stormy sea on which cotton was floating. Napoleon increased the effectiveness of cartoons, which were published as separate prints (sometimes in color), by publicizing them in the newspapers.

Napoleon devised two new means of communicating with his subjects: orders of the day and bulletins. Both dealt with military subjects, but they differed in their audiences. Bulletins were directed to the civilian population; most orders of the day spoke to the army, but on occasion they were addressed to residents of newly conquered territories.

Napoleon may not always have understood the mentality of the targets of his propaganda, but he did know the mentality of the soldiers; it was in dealing with them that he was most effective. Jerome in 1807 said that a simple word of praise or blame as Napoleon passed in front of the troops was enough to cause prodigies of valor. In his orders of the day he censured the soldiers or units who had not performed well (on the assumption that they desired his commendation), praised those who had, and inspired many to greater heights. The *Journal de l'Empire* reported that an order of the day addressed to the Bavarians in October of 1805 aroused their patriotic ardor:

> Bavarian soldiers, I put myself at the head of my army to deliver your country from unjust aggressors.
> The house of Austria wants to destroy your independence and incorporate you into its vast estates. You will be faithful to the memory of your ancestors, who . . . were never beaten and always kept their independence and political existence. . . .
> As your sovereign's good ally, I have been touched by the marks of love you have shown him in this important circumstance. I know your bravery; I flatter myself that after the first battle I shall be able to say to your prince and my people that you are worthy of fighting in the ranks of the Grand Army.

This sort of appeal was not needed until the French Revolution, when for the first time military forces were made up of citizen-soldiers rather than professionals or men crimped into service.

Orders of the day received publicity in a variety of ways.

They were always read to the soldiers by the officers. The newspapers published a good many of them, actors sometimes read them in the theaters, and many appeared in placard form.

Bulletins, labeled as such and numbered consecutively for an entire campaign, began with the 1805 campaign and continued through that of 1812 in Russia. Civilians had of course received news from generals prior to Napoleon's day, but not in this form. The bulletins contained far more than strictly military news. They gave accolades to units or individuals the Emperor considered deserving, attacked enemy rulers, and commented on many and diverse matters. The importance Napoleon attached to the bulletins is revealed by the fact that he personally wrote or edited them. And although his egocentrism was prominent, it was more for reassurance than boasting. The most famous example was Bulletin 29 of the 1812 campaign; after mentioning some of the horrors and disasters suffered by the Grand Army, Napoleon attempted to hearten the French by informing them in the last sentence that "The health of His Majesty was never better."

In his efforts to reach every available person with the bulletins, Napoleon had them read in the churches and at the theaters for the benefit particularly of the illiterate elements in the population. Until the disastrous campaign against Russia in 1812, all the bulletins appeared in the *Moniteur* and then reappeared in thousands of copies as reprints. In that year publication of bulletins became highly selective.

Napoleon leaned heavily on the big lie, especially in getting people to believe what he wanted them to on military matters. Lodi was a minor battle; Bonaparte made it seem a minor epic. Marengo came close to being a disaster; he rewrote the official account of the battle to make it appear that the fighting had developed exactly as he had planned. He had the Minister of War, Henri Clarke, inform Joseph that the art of war lay in exaggerating one's own forces and understating those of the enemy. He told Clarke,

If you speak of it [the strength of the army], you must exaggerate by doubling or trebling the number; . . . when you speak of the enemy, decrease his strength by one-half or one-third; the mind of man is such as to believe that in the long run a small number will be beaten by a big one.

Napoleon practiced his own dictum on one occasion by ordering Jerome to spread the report that he had 40,000 men when he actually had 14,000. The purpose of the bulletins and the press was to win public opinion, he said, not to serve as historical accounts. One form of falsification was to have a minister write a newspaper article and insert it as though it had emanated from a foreign country and had been excerpted from a foreign paper; another was to edit material before it was published. Napoleon also created false impressions by not mentioning adverse items while giving a large play to those representing his point of view; it is frequently more effective to ignore an item than to blast it with a withering word-fire.

The timing of various publications received considerable attention. Sometimes, for instance, Napoleon wanted publication of military news hastened so as to forestall any other account; at other times he wanted publication delayed so as to prevent the enemy's learning about developments too soon. If the public was famished for news, he gave it some; if the public was aroused, Napoleon held back. He deliberately waited several days for the Spaniards to accept the news that their King Charles IV had ceded all his rights before proclaiming Joseph king. On another occasion he told a subordinate that the Parisians were so impatient for news that every possible means should be used to expedite it. And since propaganda largely deals in stereotypes that are extremely difficult to dislodge once they are implanted, Napoleon saw the importance of setting the stereotype before the opposition could do so.

The entire governmental machinery, civilian and military, was used to distribute propaganda materials. Sometimes Joseph

Fouché, as Minister of Police, received instructions to spread news in the salons before it appeared in the papers. The *Moniteur* was read aloud in the *lycées*.

Most important among the disseminating agencies were the Ministries of Interior, Police, Foreign Affairs, and War. Napoleon's reliance on the last two indicated that his main propaganda interest lay in the diplomatic and military areas. Napoleon was the first dictator to attempt thought control in his satellite countries; of these Italy and Spain received the most propaganda attention. He was also the first to attempt to speak to people in their own language; especially in Germany there was a trend toward bilingual papers. Desirous of leaving the impression that natives were speaking to their fellow countrymen, he pretended that natives wrote materials actually composed by French officials. The satellite rulers and Berthier, the chief of staff, were largely responsible for the distribution of official pamphlets in subject territories.

Arriving at an accurate or even approximate estimate of the effectiveness of Napoleon's propaganda is extremely difficult. Yet a discussion of the propaganda would be incomplete without some mention of the attitudes of Napoleon and his enemies toward it, and the state of public opinion it helped produce.

On St. Helena Napoleon gave his opinion of the *Moniteur's* value to himself.

The *Moniteur* has been reproached for the acrimony and virulence of its notes against the enemy. But before we condemn them, we are bound to take into consideration the benefits they may have produced, the anxiety they occasionally caused to a perplexed enemy, the terror they struck in a hesitating cabinet, the stimulus they gave to our allies, the confidence and audacity they inspired in our troops.

The *Moniteurs* which are so devastating to so many reputations are invariably useful and favorable to me alone. Really talented and careful historians will write history with official documents. Now, these documents are full of me; it is their testimony that I solicit and invoke.

A more objective bit of evidence was Metternich's desire to have the allies establish an official press because of the value he had seen in the *Moniteur*. His testimony while ambassador to France remains valuable even if exaggerated:

Newspaper articles have thus so misled the public mind that everything which is said to put matters in their proper light is opposed by documents held to be official. . . . The French . . . have the game to themselves; they have only occupied an empty place by seizing the desks of the journalists. . . . The newspapers are worth to Napoleon an army of three hundred thousand men, for such a force would not overlook the interior better, or frighten foreign Powers more, than half a dozen of his paid pamphleteers.

With regard to the effect of the bulletins, Metternich wrote:

The daily bulletins which are published for the French army, and which inundate Germany and the whole of Europe, are a new invention which deserves the most serious attention. Designed less to report military facts than to mislead the public as to the spirit and principle of our government and our people, Bonaparte's cabinet thus brings itself into daily contact with all classes of society. It has given up the official style and adopted that of familiar conversation; each Bulletin brings on the scene personages whose respectability inspires confidence and men of the people who confirm what they wish to be taken for public feeling in the Austrian monarchy, and millions of readers end by accepting it as such.

Despite its exaggeration, the statement indicates that Napoleon's bulletins achieved their purpose.

Napoleon was well pleased with the success of his own invention, the orders of the day. In one of his numerous outbursts of annoyance with the propaganda activities of his subordinates he wrote:

There is no need of speaking to the army; it does not read the vain prattling of pamphlets, and one word in the order of the day would do more than a hundred volumes of Cicero and Demosthenes. One can rouse the soldiers against England without speaking to them. . . . The masses . . . should be directed without their noticing it. . . . There is no legal means of speaking to it [the army] other than through the order of the day. Everything else is intrigue and faction.

A negative but significant indication of the success of Napoleon's propaganda is the constant attacks on it by his opponents. Foreign journalists and pamphleteers regularly denounced his methods. The anti-Napoleonic French newspapers published in London vehemently pointed out the falsity of Napoleon's bulletins. Friedrich von Gentz, an Austrian statesman and no mean publicist himself, wrote a long denunciation of Napoleon's propaganda warfare.

Napoleon was not, however, completely successful in his propaganda efforts. For example, the circulation of the newspapers, on which he particularly relied, steadily fell. His desire to win middle-class backing hindered the adaptation of his message to the lower classes. The numerous diatribes in the *Moniteur* prevented that newspaper's being as effective abroad as it might have been. Napoleon himself was extremely critical of almost all the handbills he had not personally issued.

At times, as in 1804, Napoleon became extremely provoked with public opinion because it did not behave as he wanted it to:

The population of Paris is a collection of blockheads who believe the most absurd reports. . . . I respect the decisions of public opinion when they are justly formed; but it has its caprices which we ought to learn to despise. *It is the task of the government, and of those who support it, to enlighten the public, not to follow it in its meanderings* [Italics added].

Always, at all times and places, Napoleon was checking on and trying to lead public opinion, to make sure that it did not become too "capricious." The soldiers and the lower classes were the groups that remained most loyal to him, regardless of the cost of the wars. His propaganda was in general effective among the Poles and Germans under his control. It is worth noting that nobody in the areas annexed to France took the least step to throw off Napoleon's domination.

THE NAPOLEONIC REVOLUTION

If much of the material in this chapter has a familiar ring, it is because propaganda activities to a large extent still follow the paths Napoleon blazed, and contemporary propaganda is still paying him the homage of imitation. Modern dictators—thoroughly in agreement with Napoleon's statement that "It is not what is true that counts, but what people think is true"—have official and semiofficial newspapers. Armies still use orders of the day. Napoleonic bulletins have been transformed into communiqués. Napoleon made propaganda a necessary tool of modern politics and statesmanship.

Admittedly, Napoleon had not developed the technique of forming public opinion to the same degree as the dictators of our own day, nor did he have the totalitarian machinery with which to do so. He made errors that contemporary propagandists try to avoid; government propagandists today, for example, are more willing to delegate authority, to give each branch of the government a more clearly defined propaganda role, and to accept the aid of private agencies. Present-day propagandists are also more adept at fitting their techniques to particular audiences and to changing circumstances.

But Napoleon is important as being the first dictator to devote such a large share of his attention to public opinion. He spoke directly and frequently to his subjects, and not only fully exploited all existing media of communication but devised some new ones as well. He utilized the existing tools of propaganda so extensively as to make the control of military news in wartime a distinct and important arm of warfare. He did a remarkable job of conducting his propaganda along lines which would make it most effective. In the last analysis his propaganda was defeated by the course of events, against which no propaganda can successfully contend.

· IX ·

THE CATALYST OF NATIONALISM

The dominant political force of the 19th and 20th centuries has unquestionably been nationalism. It has led to a desire for national states by people within heterogeneous empires, by nationalities divided into numerous small states, and by subject colonial peoples. To a large extent the nationalism which has been so important for the last century and a half is an outgrowth of the Napoleonic period.

Nationalism had been mentioned as far back as the end of the Middle Ages. Prior to the French Revolution, however, the term was applied to what we today think of as patriotism, for then, with the possible exception of Great Britain, there were states rather than nations. This patriotism was in general linked with loyalty to the monarch, and it admitted no religious differences. The idea of nationalism seemed to be connected with popular sovereignty and civil equality; the rulers and aristocrats in power during the *ancien régime* in any country therefore naturally opposed it. One student of nationalism says it is inconceivable without preceding ideas of popular sovereignty, and without a revision of classes and castes. Only after subjects became citizens, as in the French Revolution, could modern nationalism arise.

179

THE NAPOLEONIC REVOLUTION

Several characteristics differentiated the new nationalism from the older patriotism. The most important were a feeling of mutual relationship between the government and the governed, and a feeling of community among the governed themselves. This feeling meant a desire to have a sovereign state which would include all like-minded people. (Emphasis should be placed upon the "all"; earlier nationalism or patriotism influenced only the few.) The nation needed features such as language and institutions distinguishing it from other similar groups. The strongest single tie of nationalism was language, with all its cultural derivatives, such as literature. But other factors might also enter the picture: historical tradition, geographical contiguity, political entity, religion. The new nationalism also differed from the old in that it might embrace people of more than one religion. A common sense of right and wrong was likewise important.

Nationalism is not a natural phenomenon but a cultivated sentiment which is the product of historical factors. The nation or nationality comes first, then the theory. Nationalism also demands that loyalty to the nation must take precedence over any other loyalty—that is why it can accept people of varying religious beliefs. Members of the same nation are, in common with their fellows, ready to make sacrifices, and are more willing to co-operate with one another than with other people. At the same time, of course, there is distrust of the foreigner. In Germany the poet and patriotic pamphleteer Ernst Moritz Arndt demanded the growth of a "general love among Germans" and "hatred against the crafty foreigners."

The wars of the French Revolution and Napoleon were responsible for gradually substituting nationalism for both the cosmopolitanism of the intellectuals of the Enlightenment and the parochialism of the unlettered. The threat of military invasion usually promotes social solidarity. The French, both because they were the revolutionaries and because they were the object of attack by other countries, were the first to develop a feeling of nationalism. Even before he came to power, and very effectively after his accession, Bonaparte favored this evolution. He bolstered French nationalism by centralization of activities, military service, wars—and by victories in those wars.

In his propaganda Napoleon constantly referred to France as the "great nation," rather than as the "great country." Yet he was not a nationalist for the sake of nationalism; he looked on this new force primarily as something that would foster his own cause, first by overcoming factionalism within France. In order for France to remain great, it would, of course, need a united front of its rulers and ruled; thus the role of nationalism became entwined with that of the dynasty itself. Early in the Consulate he wrote,

I want you all to rally round the mass of the people. The simple title of French citizen is worth far more than that of *royaliste, clichien, jacobin, feuillant,* or any of those thousand and one denominations which have sprung, during the past ten years, from the spirit of faction, and which are hurling the nation into an abyss from which the time has at last come to rescue it, once and for all. This is the aim of all my efforts.

Napoleon further wanted to build up the French nation so as to use it to extend his own control, aided by the beneficent influence of Revolutionary ideas. The Frenchman would of course share Napoleon's glory for the revolutionary transformation of Europe, a transformation involving such reforms as freeing peasants, establishing equality before the law, providing freedom of conscience and a uniform code, unifying the domestic market, and abolishing feudal and provincial autonomies and privileges.

On St. Helena Napoleon said, "There are in Europe more than 30 million French, 15 million Spanish, 15 million Italians, and 30 million Germans. I would have wished to make each of these peoples a single united body." This wish was pure fiction—or legend. In actuality, Napoleon did not recognize non-French nationalism or intend it to be on a par with that of France. In this realm, as in so many others, he was the classicist, the believer in one universal standard. Since France was his base, the standard would be French interests and French nationalism.

I should like a person of French extraction, even though of the tenth generation, still to find himself a Frenchman. . . . I want to raise the glory of the French name so high that it becomes the envy of all nations. I should like to see the day when, with the help of divine guidance, a Frenchman travelling throughout Europe could always find himself at home.[1]

Thus for France the national ideal was not to be contained within its borders.

Napoleon's attitude toward non-French nationalism resulted in part from his misunderstanding and underestimating it. To him the spirit of nationalism, when it occurred abroad, seemed far less strong, and therefore less dangerous, than religious or political feelings and beliefs. Napoleon thought that people could be won away from national allegiance and united in a great international state.[2] It therefore did not greatly matter to him that nationalism was incompatible with the imperialism he was advocating, and the universal empire of which he dreamed. Especially after 1810 the Napoleonic empire was the negation of nationality outside France. It was in that year that he wrote Eugene:

My principle is *France first*. . . . It would be short-sighted not to recognize that Italy owes her independence to France—that it was won by French blood and French victories, that it must not be misused. . . . Make your motto too—*France first*.

That later generations of Frenchmen, who claimed Napoleon was merely defending their natural frontiers, should have con-

[1] Quoted in Bernard Schwartz (ed.), *The Code Napoleon and the Common Law World*. New York: New York University Press, 1956, p. 107.

[2] But this international state by conquest would differ greatly from the cosmopolitanism of the Enlightenment, for France would hold first rank.

sidered him a nationalist is not surprising. What is surprising is that for half a century or more after his fall liberals in Italy, Poland, Belgium, and even in western and southern Germany and in Spain, tended to forget his desire for domination and empire and to look on him as the defender of nationalities against reactionary kings.

And he did bring to life or resurrect German, Italian, Polish, Southern Slav, and Spanish nationalism. Of these, only two proved to be advantageous to him.

The first was Italian nationalism, to which Napoleon made concessions. He wanted it to be at the *juste milieu,* sufficiently strong to serve as a support against the *ancien régime* rulers, but not powerful enough to threaten his own plans. In addition to the reforms he usually introduced in subject areas, he gave the Italians a flag and an army. Army officers returned from the wars nationalistic minded. The mere fact that he reduced the number of states on the peninsula to three, including the part incorporated into France, tended to induce nationalistic feelings and pride on the part of the Italians. This was more particularly true because one of those parts was titled the Italian Republic from 1802 to 1805 and the Kingdom of Italy thereafter. Napoleon encouraged the exclusive use of the Tuscan dialect, the literary language of Italy. But his image as a promoter of Italian nationalism was dimmed by other actions, such as awarding Italian principalities to his marshals and other high French officials or making such annexations to France as that of Parma in 1806, Tuscany in 1808, and the Papal States in 1809. Much of the later Italian national sentiment was a reaction against rather than a continuation of the Napoleonic regime.

The other people whose nationalistic impulses served Napoleon was the Poles, who had been divided before and during the French Revolution among their neighbors, Russia, Prussia, and Austria. Napoleon's actions led the Poles to hope, and Tsar Alexander of Russia to fear, that he was going to establish a

Kingdom of Poland.[3] The Poles remained loyal followers of Napoleon to the end of his reign. Yet at the same time that he led the Poles to believe their support of him would be rewarded at some unspecified future date, Napoleon was very careful never to promise them a kingdom.

In a third area, the engendered nationalism proved to be neither beneficial nor detrimental to Napoleon. This was the case in the Illyrian provinces, which were formed from the Dalmatian holdings taken away from Austria after the campaigns of 1805 and 1809. For the first time since the 14th century various Southern Slav peoples were grouped together. Croatian and Slovenian received the status of official languages. From such facts as these sprang the Southern Slav nationalist movement of the 19th and 20th centuries that brought about the formation of Yugoslavia following World War I and Titoism after World War II.

Nationalism that arose elsewhere, though springing partly from the history of the areas and partly from imitation of France, came mainly as a reaction to Napoleon's domination. As Gneisenau, later the famous reformer of the Prussian army, stated after the crushing defeat of Jena:

> The Revolution has set in action the national energy of the entire French people . . . thereby abolishing the former relationship of the states to one another and the balance of power. If the other states wish to re-establish this balance, they must open and use these resources. They must take over the results of the Revolution and so gain the double advantage of being able to place their entire national energies in opposition to the enemy.[4]

Even though it opposed him, and its development surprised him, Napoleon must be given credit—or blame—for the arousing of national consciousness in such places as Germany and Spain. In the words of Ernest Lavisse, "It is the Revolution he serves, in

---

[3] See Chapter II.

[4] Quoted in Boyd Shafer, *Nationalism: Myth and Reality*. New York: Harcourt, Brace, 1955, p. 138.

spite of himself and against himself, when, oppressing Europe because such is his pleasure, he awakens the soul of the Spanish and German peoples." His invasion of Russia undoubtedly increased national solidarity there also.

There is no questioning the national motivation in the Spaniards' fight against Napoleon, but one must be careful not to exaggerate it. The tendency to do so frequently stems directly or indirectly from Madame de Staël, who wrote that in Spain Napoleon "was faced with national resistance, the only kind he could not deal with by diplomacy or bribes. . . . He never understood that a war might be a crusade. . . . He never reckoned with the one power that no arms could overcome—the enthusiasm of a whole people"

Some facts do back up this interpretation. Madrid revolted against the French on May 2, 1808. Although Murat quickly and severely suppressed the uprising, May 2 still remains a Spanish national holiday. Guerrilla resistance increased steadily. Though there were in Spain no theoretical nationalist writings, there was an actual nationalist rebellion, or war for independence, against Bonapartist control. Here for the first time Napoleon seemed to be fighting a people rather than rulers.

This traditional interpretation of the Spanish fighting, though accurate to a point, overlooks several important factors. Dynastic loyalty in Spain was far stronger than in France. The religious element also played a large role, for the peasants were greatly influenced by their parish priests, and it must be remembered that Napoleon at the time was having difficulty with the Pope. The guerrillas were at least as imbued with local patriotism for their province or locality as they were with a feeling of being Spanish.

The uprising was a good deal less spontaneous than Madame de Staël would make it appear. The revolt against Napoleon did not start immediately, and it began in those provinces of Spain which the French did not invade. The nobility and clergy in these areas explained to the masses why they had to be called to

arms because of what was taking place elsewhere. These dominant classes unquestionably turned patriotic feeling to their own
special interests; the people were far from unanimous in their
answer to the call. The role of the regular army was considerable.
The defeat of General Pierre Dupont at Bailén, which caused a
sensation throughout Europe because it showed the French were
not invincible, was the work of Spanish regulars, not of a popular
uprising. If it had not been for Wellington's forces, the Spanish
guerrilla resistance would in all probability eventually have
collapsed.

Still another feature was the fact that the peasants were fighting for their own food, for the French were in the habit of living
off the countryside, requisitioning or seizing supplies from the
peasants. This aspect of the fighting naturally grew more important as the campaign became more drawn out.

It was Germany, rather than Spain, which furnished the prime
example of a nationalism engendered by the Napoleonic period.
More advanced culturally than Spain and with more capable
leaders, it forged in a short space of time the most important non-
French nationalism on the Continent. German developments
therefore deserve a more extensive account than those which
took place elsewhere.

Napoleon refused to believe there were people who felt themselves to be Germans; in Germany he saw only herds, not thinking people. In this brusque statement he dismissed any ideas of
German nationalist feeling: "Rubbish. I have made short work of
these fancies. . . . In Germany the common people want to be
protected against the great ones; the great ones want to govern
after their pleasures." Madame de Staël, Napoleon's constant
critic and a faithful interpreter of the German mood, said that
the Germans had no national spirit in 1804 but did have a few
years later, and that Napoleon had only himself to blame for the
change. Goethe in 1830 confirmed her statement:

We have no city, nay we have no country of which we could decidedly say—Here is Germany! If we inquire in Vienna, the answer is—This is Austria! and if in Berlin—This is Prussia! Only when we tried to get rid of the French, sixteen years ago, was Germany everywhere.[5]

In Germany Napoleon's drastic reduction in the number of states, started with the *Reichsdeputationshauptschluss* and continued with the organization of the Confederation of the Rhine, unwittingly promoted a feeling of nationalism. The French author François René Chateaubriand stated the matter well:

Napoleon thought that by effacing so many frontiers and drawing all these strategic roads he was merely tracing the way from his barracks; in fact he was opening the road to a fatherland.[6]

In destroying the Holy Roman Empire he cleared away a thousand-year-old obstacle to the development of nationality and a national spirit. As the American historian James Harvey Robinson wrote:

Napoleon, in a somewhat incidental and left-handed fashion, did so much to promote the progress both of democratic institutions and of nationality in Western Europe that he may, in a sense, be regarded as the putative father of them both. . . . He is the founder of modern Germany.[7]

The execution of a single, ordinary man in 1806 contributed greatly to the feeling of oneness which transcended the bounds of individual German states. Johann Palm, a bookseller at Nürnberg, was executed by the French for selling the anonymous pamphlet *Germany in Her Deepest Humiliation*. The German nationalism evoked by such tracts obviously turned against the

[5] Quoted in J. M. Thompson, *Napoleon Bonaparte*. New York: Oxford University Press, 1952, p. 355.

[6] Napoleon's actions may also be interpreted as a continuation of the French policy of keeping Germany divided, setting up a third state as a counterweight to Austria and Prussia.

[7] Cited in Louis L. Snyder, *The Meaning of Nationalism*. New Brunswick, N.J.: Rutgers University Press, 1954, p. 81.

French. But German national consciousness was still confined to a minority of the people.[8]

German nationalism differed from that of France and Great Britain in being less rational and in putting more stress on the mystical concept of the "folk." It looked upon the nation as a living being created by the unconscious action of the *Volksgeist* ("spirit of the people"). This made it more conservative than English or French nationalism, for it looked back to an idealized past that many German nationalists unrealistically thought might be restored in the future.

The writings of cultural nationalists cleared the path for the activity of the political nationalists. The defeat of Prussia in 1806 led some German writers to fear that French would again become the literary language of Germany. The poet and dramatist Heinrich von Kleist asked, "Who knows whether in a hundred years anybody will still speak German in this country?" Friedrich Schiller in 1805 added the uprising of William Tell and the Germanic Swiss to the national heritage. The significance of the splendid literature of national awakening can scarcely be overemphasized.

Political nationalists shortly followed in the footsteps of the cultural ones. The most important of them for our purposes was Johann Fichte, a philosopher and teacher. While the French were occupying Berlin, he delivered his series of *Addresses to the German Nation*. In them he advocated education as the only means of fully developing the latent nationalism of the German people. (In Germany as well as in France earlier and in Russia later, the thought prevailed that the primary function of public education was to prepare the pupils for membership in the

[8] It should not be too surprising that the masses were primarily motivated by other considerations. For example, in rural German areas the peasants, customarily and traditionally docile, would tend to do what the neighboring noble desired. Public opinion was the product of, and tended to be the possession of, a relative handful.

national society.) Fichte also stated, in nationalistic fashion, that no other nation could compare with the German, telling his students, "To have character and to be a German undoubtedly mean the same thing." Although French agents were in the hall as he spoke, they did not interfere as they thought his ideas so intellectual as to be harmless.

All the nationalistic elements in Germany rallied to Prussia. Except for it and Austria, the German states met one of two fates: they were annexed to France or they became satellites of Napoleon as members of the Confederation of the Rhine (and in two cases ruled by relatives of Napoleon, Murat in Berg and Jerome in Westphalia).

The position of Austria was anomalous. The Austrian Empire included many different peoples governed by a German minority. Emperor Francis I, realizing that his state was dynastic and feudal, never favored nationalism. (At most he was on occasion neutral on the matter.) But fear of Napoleon led other high Austrian officials in 1808 and 1809 to favor an appeal to the German nationalism common to Austria and the other states of the former Holy Roman Empire. The Austrian official Friedrich Gentz once remarked, "If Germany should become united, then we can say farewell to Russia, can see England fighting its glorious fight on a sure and grand basis, and can laugh at all the threats of France." Similarly Friedrich Schlegel, hired by the Austrian government to write patriotic propaganda, asked, "How much longer will you be crushed under the heels of a proud conqueror? . . . Awaken, Germans, from the stupor of shame and ignominy." After the Treaty of Schönbrunn, however, the Austrian Emperor Francis replaced the pro-German nationalists with more conventional men.

It was while the nationalists were administering Austrian affairs that the Austrian government encouraged the revolt led by Andreas Hofer in the Tyrol. This uprising is commonly interpreted as being nationalistic; but despite Hofer's being inspired by the guerrilla warfare in Spain, his uprising was a protest against the rule of another German state, Bavaria, to which Napoleon had given the Tyrol by the Treaty of Pressburg. The rebels were largely peasants, who pillaged and maltreated the *bourgeoisie*. Hofer's revolt, therefore, though patriotic, illustrates the importance of class and group grievances rather than of nationalism.

Nationalism was admittedly less important in Austria than in Prussia. Weak as Prussia was after 1806, it thus offered the only hope to those Germans who wanted to establish a national state within the confines of the former Holy Roman Empire. The very fact of its weakness was important in Prussia's assumption of leadership; defeated countries and armies generally do more self-examination than those that fare well. Prussia was more than defeated: it was humiliated and had lost half its territory.

Prussia's, and Germany's, humiliation led in 1806 to the formation at the University of Königsberg of the *Tugendbund* (League of Virtue), dedicated to liberating Germany from the oppressor. This and other manifestations of nationalism were opposed by the conservatives, who feared that nationalism would destroy attachment to the individual states and to the old, landed aristocracy. Although the sentiment of local patriotism, of particularism, was still very strong, there was a growing demand among the liberals for a truly national state.

Prussia was fortunate in having the services of a number of outstanding reformers at this time. The Freiherr Stein set the tone, followed by such men as Karl von Hardenberg in administration, Scharnhorst and Count August von Gneisenau in the army, and Wilhelm von Humboldt in education. In general, the Prussian reformers between 1807 and 1813 aimed at a united German state, not merely the regeneration of Prussia. Hardenberg, for example, announced in 1810 that he was determined "not to perpetuate provincialism, but rather to introduce nationalism." One reason for their actions, and it again reveals the influence of

Napoleon, was that the French had introduced their type of social organization into Warsaw and Westphalia, whose proximity might well cause discontent in and emigration from Prussia.

Without Napoleon, reform in Germany would have been much slower and less peaceful. The defeat of Prussia, the collapse of the Prussian army at Jena, forced even those opposed to any change to realize that the army had to be revamped. Reform of the army had first priority. As the discussion in Chapter II pointed out, the goal was a national army. But Prussian government and society were so militaristic, the army organization so closely interwoven with the whole social fabric, that military changes were bound to necessitate reforms in other spheres.

In education, where the reforms were lastingly successful, the goal was a national system of education. The principles of the Swiss reformer Johann Pestalozzi were applied in the elementary schools, and a Pestalozzian normal school was established at Königsberg in East Prussia. Technical instruction was encouraged. Gymnasia were established, and leaving examinations were inaugurated so as to tie together secondary schools and the universities. To cap this structure, the renowned University of Berlin was founded with a distinguished faculty.

The Prussian reforms were not revolutionary, for they had none of the egalitarian spirit. Although the caste system was to disappear, the Junkers were to retain their social authority. Power was to remain in the hands of the king. But for the first time in Prussia the Junker monopoly on landed property was broken; in exchange, the Junkers were free to enter professions formerly closed to them. Serfdom was abolished; peasants could henceforth freely move, marry, engage in any occupation they chose. East Prussia, where 30,000 peasants became proprietors, was the first province to effect this reform, in August of 1807; in October, Stein, in the famous Edict of Emancipation, extended abolition of serfdom to the entire country. It provided that the peasants would be free as of November 11, 1810. But in other respects the edict was ambiguous. A compromise solution was reached on peasant security: instead of a general law, there were provincial edicts appearing in the years 1808 to 1810; peasants holding new tenures, none older than 1752, were subject to eviction; the lord could take back older holdings only if he granted hereditary leases on an equal but less subdivided acreage.

The primary motive behind the agrarian reform was fiscal and economic, to benefit the treasury, the king, and the nobility. This helps explain why the peasant's lot, though juridically better, was not so economically. The peasant lost a goodly portion, about half, of the land he had formerly cultivated. The lord no longer had to care for him in time of adversity, but the lord still administered the village, and the nobility retained all of their privileges except that of a monopoly on land.

Yet the abolition of serfdom, the breaking up of the Junker land monopoly, and the opening of all occupations to all persons were prerequisites to any modernization of Prussia. Only after these developments could modern social classes replace the older castes.

Economic reforms were, thanks to Stein, most far-reaching in East Prussia. There he abolished several corporations, suppressed banalities,[9] and let the peasants buy and sell in the town market. As this last reform greatly diminished excise tax receipts, Stein got the provincial diet (*Landtag*) to vote an income tax. Hardenberg had to replace this in 1810, however, with an increased stamp tax and sales taxes because of its unpopularity.

The government of the cities was reformed in lasting fashion by an ordinance of November 19, 1808, the work of Stein just five days before Napoleon's opposition forced him from office. The cities received more self-government; each one had an elected

[9] Banality was the term for a payment for compulsory use of facilities furnished by the lord, especially his mill and bake-oven.

assembly, which chose a magistrature. All citizens who met certain property requirements could vote.

As a result of these reforms and developments, men for the first time thought of Germany as a political entity facing the foreigner.

Although Napoleon did not have such a result in mind, he nonetheless helped create several nations existing today—among them Germany, Italy, and Yugoslavia. In this respect his regime had a threefold influence. His territorial arrangements promoted the awakening of nationalities. Furthermore, by reforms outside France Napoleon created political and social conditions which fostered political nationalism. Although he did not seem to realize it would happen, the principles of the French Revolution produced elsewhere in Europe the same feelings of national unity as in France. Changes that did much to facilitate nationalism included the creation of administrative hierarchies and the forming of citizen armies.

But Napoleon's most powerful stimulus to nationalism came from his conquests. Foreign occupiers are seldom if ever popular with the common people, and French exactions did more to make Napoleon unpopular in Germany than all the work of propagandists for nationalism. Even backward Illyria, unable to understand or appreciate many of the reforms, responded to their cost with a nationalistic reaction. Out of fear and hate, many European peoples came to desire national unity, national independence, and such national institutions as a citizen army and a system of public education. National languages became more important in many areas, and a start was made toward transforming cultural into political nationalism.

Thus Napoleon's greatest contribution to nationalism was a negative one. But this fact did not lessen his impact on European political life of the 19th and 20th centuries.

· X ·

THE LEGACY

"The Napoleonic Revolution." By definition a revolution is a successful movement, effecting far-reaching changes in a short space of time. Napoleon's legacy of change had three components: firstly, those items he wanted to bequeath to posterity; secondly, the unforeseen outgrowths of his policies; and, thirdly, the changed conditions brought into being as a reaction against his regime.

A key to his entire policy is contained in the proclamation of the three consuls on December 15, 1799, slightly more than a month after they had taken office: "Citizens, the Revolution is stabilized on the principles which began it." With the exception of fathering the Civil Code, Napoleon perhaps gloried more in his reputation as consolidator of the Revolution than in any other one title. Undoubtedly he realized his debt to the Revolution. As one historian has said, the Consulate and Empire accepted without benefit of inventory the main results of the Revolution, and in this spirit established the foundations of a new order. Even while Napoleon reconciled the ideas of the Revolution with some from the Bourbon monarchy, he consolidated the work of the Revolution in putting an end to the complex of institutions which constituted the *ancien régime*.

This task of consolidation made Napoleon a conservative in France, desirous of keeping the gains of the Revolution, but a revolutionary in *ancien-régime* areas abroad. In France it meant that he retained the semblance of universal suffrage and of a constitution. Although he had an enlightened despot's mentality with respect to economic activities, he maintained a façade of economic liberalism: keeping the Le Chapelier law in force, he did not permit the formation of associations, and he did not permit the re-establishment of internal customs. (His desire for unity would in any case have forbidden such internal division in the country.) The educational system he established fulfilled the idea of the Revolutionaries for a national system—while also serving Napoleon's purpose of indoctrination. He consolidated the gains of the Revolution in equality (at least initially), in legal and administrative unity, and in having careers open to talent.

Although we have been speaking of the Revolution as an integral movement, the Revolution had several phases. Napoleon carried on these differing aspects in varying degrees. But in one respect in which they were consistent, he strayed from the norm: The Revolutionaries of every phase from National Assembly to Directory believed in and advocated representative institutions; although Napoleon retained such organs of government, he never allowed them much latitude, and from time to time he restricted their role. He could not reconcile Revolutionary thought with the re-establishment of an autocracy.

In his triumphant march across Europe, Napoleon called himself a "soldier of the Revolution." The reforms which had been instituted in France he carried in his knapsack for every place where he obtained control. This policy is demonstrated in his letter to Louis (cited in Chapter IV) instructing him to put the Napoleonic Code into effect in Holland—and without any changes. (Here Napoleon reveals himself as the classicist, the man who believed in one universal standard.) Extending the reforms meant that serfdom disappeared from many parts of Europe which had not seen fit to abolish it at the time of the French Revolution. For example, western and southern Germany were henceforth free of that blight, as was Italy. The Napoleonic Code also made its way into the Duchy of Warsaw, where it was popular enough for Alexander I of Russia to permit its basic features, such as equality before the law, to continue even after Napoleon's downfall.

In Spain, the French hold was never strong enough to implant French customs firmly, and the reforms of Napoleon did not last beyond the time of Joseph. But the ideals did not die out. Some bourgeois Spanish liberals incorporated them into a constitution in 1812. They made their mark again in the revolutionary movement of 1820–23, when the Spanish constitution of 1812 became the watchword of the revolutionaries everywhere.

The lasting quality of Napoleon's reforms outside France was in direct ratio to the length of time French control had been in effect and to the weakness of the local governments. In the areas annexed before 1804, the Revolutionary changes were put into effect as a whole. Italy was more profoundly transformed than any other part of Europe. The stronger the local governments were, the more able they were to overthrow Napoleonic institutions after his military defeat. But only rarely did the reaction upset the civil principles which to Napoleon were so important. Even in Naples King Ferdinand did not abolish the Civil Code or re-establish feudal rights when he returned. All the reactionary forces of Europe combined were not strong enough to restore things as they had been before the outbreak of the French Revolution. They could not, in particular, undo the many-faceted social change that had been set in motion.

One aspect of this change in France—one there was no serious attempt to uproot even though Louis XVIII revised it extensively —was the Legion of Honor, created in 1802, but given a complete organization only in 1804. Bonaparte cynically remarked, "It is by baubles that men are led." He realized that the people were avid for decorations; not one of the *cahiers* of 1789 had demanded the abolition of honorific distinctions. With the Legion of Honor he created a different type of nobility, a nobility based on ability, open to anybody who had, in the view of the government, made a sufficient contribution to society. Depending on their rank, members received annual stipends ranging from 250 to 5,000 francs.

The Legion of Honor was not very popular at the time of its institution: it received a favorable vote of only 14–10 in the Council of State, 50–38 in the Tribunate (after amendments), and 166–110 in the Legislative Body. It was thought to be a reactionary step, and indeed it did look back to the *ancien régime*. Though it was Bonaparte's first step toward a hierarchical organization of society, it could also be argued that the Legion did not violate the principle of equality, since anybody might be appointed a member. Despite its initial unpopularity, its insignia soon became all the rage, and by the time of Napoleon's downfall the Legion had become so popular that even the republicans were clamoring to be named to it.

Other measures foreshadowed the return of a privileged class. These included the creation of senatorships, re-establishment of princely titles for members of the imperial family, and granting of such titles as *Monseigneur* and *Most Serene Highness*. Finally came creation of a new hereditary nobility with sufficient wealth to maintain itself. Rank was initially based on the holder's civil or military functions. This social change definitely violated the principle of equality; after having undermined the liberty of the Revolution on the grounds that the French desired equality more, Napoleon had proceeded to undermine equality. Creation of the new nobility indirectly favored later democracy, for the struggle between the old and the new aristocracies permitted democracy to profit from their differences.

Since the most capable class of society was the *bourgeoisie*, it is not surprising that Napoleon aimed most of his program at improving its lot. He contributed greatly toward its continued rise. Both legal and economic measures—for example, the legal codes and the stimulation of industry—tended toward this result. (But the stronger the *bourgeoisie* became in France, the more it turned away from the regime.) Although politically the *bourgeoisie* in France was temporarily eclipsed by the aristocracy after 1814, it came into its own with the revolution of 1830. The succeeding regime is frequently known as the "bourgeois monarchy"; the social basis on which it was built was laid during the Napoleonic period.

Napoleon also aided the rise of the middle classes outside France. It is no accident that the *bourgeoisie* was most attached, and the nobility most hostile, to his regime. Introduction of the Civil Code, with its equal treatment of all individuals, and centralization of government with its implied elimination of feudal rights, contributed to this development. Even in so backward an area as Calabria, in southernmost Italy, the Napoleonic period effected a temporary displacement of the aristocracy by the *bourgeoisie*.

A fourth aspect of the social revolution was the improvement in the legal status of the peasants, a natural corollary of the breakdown of feudal privileges. In some localities, however, the nobility retained most of its rights, and the social reform remained incomplete. Outside France (in France the Revolutionaries rather than Napoleon must receive the credit, though Napoleon maintained their work) the farmer was not better off economically; but the new legal status was a prerequisite to later economic developments, which gave a wider choice of activity to families in the low economic brackets.

Finally, in the social sphere, the Napoleonic influence accounted for the improved status and better treatment of Jews. Although they were not treated the same everywhere, they had the right to worship (at least in private) and in some cases became full-fledged citizens. In some regions they preferred not to be assimilated, and to pay tribute rather than serve in the army.

Like most dictators, Napoleon frequently relied on public works to distract the people from politics and to leave lasting monuments to his regime. He constructed public works as far away as Illyria, and conceived numerous ones for Rome, which he called his "second capital." But it was his first capital, Paris, on which he concentrated.

Napoleon thought of Paris as the cultural center of at least Europe, and perhaps the world, just as it was the political center of the French Empire. He therefore looted all possible areas to make the Louvre a world art center. Among the arts, Napoleon was especially interested in architecture. Buildings he commissioned had a classical inspiration, and his principle seemed to be that "what is large is beautiful." In addition to the complete transformation of the earlier parish church of the Madeleine, which could now be mistaken for a Greek temple, and the Roman-style Arc de Triomphe de l'Étoile (both finished by the July Monarchy after 1830), Napoleon was responsible for the Bourse, the Arc de Triomphe du Carrousel, the façade of the Chamber of Deputies, numerous fountains, four bridges (those of the Arts, of Austerlitz, of Saint-Louis, and of Jéna), the Vendôme Column, and the courtyard and the Rivoli wing of the Louvre. The rue de Rivoli (finished by Baron Haussmann under Napoleon III), the rue de la Paix (initially called "rue Napoléon" because it was to be the finest in Paris), and the rue de Castiglione all date from the imperial epoch. So do the squares of the Bastille and Saint-Sulpice. In addition, Napoleon acquired the terrain which made possible the later Trocadero.

Alongside his esthetic works Napoleon instituted certain features necessary for the modernization of Paris: sidewalks, house numbers, two miles of new *quais*, a water supply, sewers, a fire department, new markets and slaughter houses. Napoleon also replaced the eccentric street names of the Revolution. In 1811 he wrote his Minister of the Interior, Montalivet, that the four most important contributions he had made to Paris were to bring it water by building a canal from the Ourcq River, the new markets at Les Halles, the wine market, and the slaughter houses.

Under Napoleon the government, largely to keep him informed, started publication in 1811 of a *Journal général de l'imprimerie et de la librairie* (General Journal of Printing and Bookselling). Under the title *Bibliographie de la France* it has been published ever since, an inestimable service to researchers and booksellers. Another lasting benefit was the definition of the rules of literary property, equivalent to copyright law, by a decree of February 5, 1810. The rules laid down then lasted until 1866, and they accounted in part for the intellectual flowering of France after 1815. An author or his widow could retain rights as long as either lived, and the children could have them for an additional twenty years, ten more than had been conceded during the Revolution.

Even while on campaign in Russia, Napoleon issued theater regulations which basically remained in effect a century after his downfall. The decree drawn up in Moscow laid down the organization of the Théâtre-Français and stipulated that the Superintendent of Spectacles should appoint the committee which would decide whether the Théâtre would perform a particular play.

The Convention had earlier organized public welfare so as to eliminate poverty, vagabondage, and begging. Under Napoleon there was greater centralization of activity. Each *arrondissement* had a "central committee of charity" presided over by the prefect or subprefect. Public soup kitchens were organized to help the needy, but in general the regime favored private rather than public charity, by charitable societies like those of the *ancien régime*. In 1808 begging was forbidden, and the penal code of 1810 organized its judicial repression. Foundlings and orphans were assisted by legislation in 1811.

Napoleon also paid some slight attention to public health. He laid down the requirements for a person to be a pharmacist or a physician. The government favored vaccination against smallpox, and it made a feeble attempt to increase the number of midwives so as to raise the percentage of live births. Chaptal, as Minister of the Interior, started on a system of hospitals, each of which was to have schools for nurses, midwives, and obstetricians. It was the first organized public enterprise of its kind in the world.

It would be very difficult to say in which area Napoleon's impact was the greatest. But on any list of the fields which he consciously sought to change, government and administration would rank high. Even the rulers who opposed him accepted, in lesser or greater degree, his concept of a modern state—centralized, acting directly on individuals without intermediaries, and treating these individuals as citizens rather than as subjects. Napoleon in his centralization and in his police force introduced the military system into government. His Council of State, composed as it was of experts, might be considered the forerunner of today's legislative reference agencies which draft bills. It was appointed by and responsible to the chief executive. Although several of his administrative institutions caused murmurings when he established them, almost all survived him; moreover, they have served as props for the government of France in times of instability. The changes of Cabinet in the Third and Fourth Republics, averaging approximately one every six months from 1870 to 1958, were serious; but they were less devastating than a similar number of changes would have been in England, for example, because of the stable bureaucracy which Napoleon provided for France.

Napoleon had maintained at least the fiction of a constitutional form of government; Louis XVIII realized that he also had to grant a constitution if he was to have any popular support. His Constitutional Charter of 1814, whose preamble stated that it was Louis' gift to France, was drawn up by former functionaries of Napoleon. It retained for the French the land settlement of the Revolution, equality before the law, equality of taxation, personal liberty, freedom of the press and of religion, the Legion of Honor, the court system, and the Napoleonic nobility. The Additional Act granted by Napoleon in 1815 closely resembled Louis XVIII's Constitutional Charter, and both made outstanding concessions to the *bourgeoisie*. Both, for example, retained the system of electoral colleges. Men could be members of these colleges only if they paid a large sum in direct taxes; and to be eligible for the elective house of the legislature, individuals had to pay an amount imposed on only a few wealthy individuals. The inviolability of property was a great boon to the *bourgeoisie* and a source of reassurance to those who had profited from the Revolution, particularly in the buying of land.

Along with the idea of a constitution went that of ratifying governmental changes by plebiscite. Although Napoleon did not initiate the use of the plebiscite, that being the work of the Revolutionaries, he used it frequently enough to set a precedent which was adopted by later rulers. (It should be remembered that a plebiscite is not necessarily a genuine consultation of the people.)

Many of Napoleon's other institutions were retained. The University of France continued to supervise the education of the nation's youth. The Concordat ruled relations between the French government and the Papacy for ninety years after Napoleon's disappearance from power. The Bank of France continued both as servant and master of the state. The various Napoleonic legal codes remained in effect. The police remained as it had been under Napoleon—and for a time the same man even served as Minister of Police under Louis XVIII. Prefects continued to be appointed by the executive arm of the national government.

In another momentous bequest to the 19th century, and even to the 20th, Napoleon revolutionized the methods of warfare. Because his operations were bigger and more extensive than earlier ones, logistics became a more important teammate of strategy. Putting into effect as an art the principles of warfare advocated by preceding military thinkers and field commanders, he forced other countries to be imitative as the only hope of success. One of history's minor ironies is that France abandoned conscription under the Bourbon restoration, at a time when other countries were adopting it so as to compete with the France of Napoleon.

Many of the lasting results of Napoleon's reign were obviously not sought by him. Some were natural outgrowths of projects he initiated; others were results unrelated to any aim Napoleon had in mind.

One form taken by the reaction against Napoleon's despotism was a renewed popularity for English parliamentarianism; even the French Constitution of 1814 showed its influence. Yet, because of Napoleon, British repression of the lower classes lasted longer than would otherwise have been the case. Even prior to the outbreak of the French Revolution there had been a demand for reform of Parliament; William Pitt the Younger as Prime Minister had favored it. The Revolution and then Napoleon, who was viewed as the embodiment of the Revolution, brought a postponement of parliamentary reform until 1832. Instead of being inclined to concede any reform, the ruling upper classes in Britain adopted a policy of severely repressing any untoward activity. Thus, unmoved by the widespread suffering caused by the economic dislocation following the wars against Napoleon, the British government took harsh measures against the massive demonstrations of the discontented working class. The upper *bourgeoisie* and the aristocracy felt that their successful conclusion of the wars proved the perfection of the existing political and social systems of Britain; anybody desiring change was therefore irrationally dangerous.

A brief Russian revolutionary movement also resulted from the

Napoleonic period, especially from the Hundred Days venture. Napoleon's return from Elba, and his welcome in France, led the Allies to include in the Second Treaty of Paris a clause providing for an army of occupation in France. It was precisely the Russian officers stationed in this army who, having become acquainted with some of the liberal aspects of western Europe, later organized or joined secret societies aimed at obtaining reforms within Russia. After the tsarist government of Alexander I repressed the societies, some of these army men revolted against the regime. Rather than merely attempting a palace revolt, they were trying to effect a political program; hence their appellation, "the first Russian revolutionaries." Although they were defeated, and even though nobody directly carried on their revolutionary activities, they became an inspiration for Russian populist revolutionaries of the last third of the 19th century and the early part of the 20th.

Another result of his rule undesired by Napoleon was a widening of the gap between British industry and that of the Continent. London became the world's busiest commercial entrepôt. British capitalism was more dynamic than ever.

Napoleon's wars brought about the settlement of 1815, with the rulers hoping to return to the "good old days" before 1792; but, try as they would, they were unable to revert to the situation at the outbreak of the Revolutionary wars. As was true with the Napoleonic reforms, territorial changes could not be ignored or suppressed.

The diplomats had several principles in mind in formulating the peace treaties and the Final Act of the Congress of Vienna, but not all of them could be carried out. The first was legitimacy, putting back into power the families which had been ruling in 1789. Complete fulfillment of this principle was obviously impossible because of the second principle, compensation: states which lost territory in one place would be given territory somewhere else. The latter principle did not apply, of course, to the ecclesiastical or city states of Germany which had been used as a compensation to the territorial rulers.

The third principle was that of a return to the balance of power, the dominant idea or policy guiding European foreign relations for almost three centuries and especially important in the 17th and 18th centuries. This was directly contrary to the purpose of Napoleon; he wanted to make France so strong that it, alone, would be able to maintain peace. The balance of power principle, a natural reaction to Napoleon, led the other countries to strengthen those states which might serve as buffers against a France once again offensive-minded.

But the Congress of Vienna could not find a lasting solution to the problems of Poland and Belgium, of Germany and Italy, because it disregarded the feeling of nationality which Napoleon had stimulated by his reforms and territorial changes, or which had arisen in reaction to him. The Congress agreed to replace the defunct Holy Roman Empire with a German Confederation having virtually the same geographical limits. The number of German states was never again, however, raised to any such fantastic total as had existed before the outbreak of the Revolution; in 1815 there were fewer than forty. A Congress Kingdom of Poland, formed from the Duchy of Warsaw, became a part of the Russian Empire.

A natural result of Napoleon's reign was a Europe-wide distrust of the French as a warlike people, and a desire to hold France in check. Looking backward, as treaty makers—not without some justification—are prone to do, those of 1815 decided to surround France with strong states so as to make more unlikely any renewed aggression on its part. The Kingdom of the Netherlands (for it was now a kingdom) obtained the former Austrian Netherlands so as to be able to form a strong bastion against French expansion toward the north. Switzerland was enlarged and its neutrality proclaimed; surely an aggressive France would not risk the displeasure of all Europe by violating its neutrality.

The Kingdom of Sardinia gained the rest of Savoy so as to hold back France in the southeast. And Prussia gained extensive holdings along the Rhine. (It also got three-fifths of Saxony in return for its surrender of Polish-inhabited territory to Russia.) Since all of Prussia's gains were German and its losses non-German, it became more predominantly a German state, and was therefore in a better position to assume at a later date the leadership in the unification of Germany.

On the map of 1815 France was smaller than at the beginning of Napoleon's fifteen years in power. The Second Treaty of Paris, between the Allies and France after the Hundred Days, reduced its borders to those of 1789 plus the former Papal possession of Avignon. This meant that France lost the gains made by the treaties of the War of the First Coalition, in Italy and west of the Rhine. Napoleon should not receive full and exclusive condemnation for these losses as the Directory had pursued a foreign policy which brought into being a second coalition before Bonaparte assumed power. The fact remains, however, that Napoleon's regime cost France territory, and that his return to France in the Hundred Days cost it more than would otherwise have been the case. France was no longer the *grande nation*, the greatest nation in Europe.

These territorial changes were added to those effected earlier in Europe as a result of Napoleon's actions. Sweden now had Norway, because Russia's ante of Norway had proved more attractive than Napoleon's bid of the return of Finland. Finland, a part of Sweden in 1789, was a part of Russia after 1809. Russia had also gained Bessarabia from the Ottoman Empire.

The blocking of action can be as important as pushing it through. Such was the case with Napoleon's preventing Russian annexation of the Dardanelles.

Other changes Napoleon had not contemplated came overseas —changes described by some historians as more important than developments in Europe. Britain was able to extend its colonial

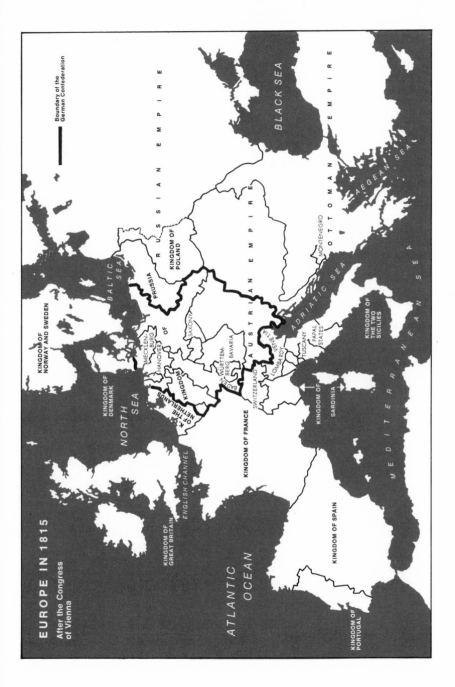

EUROPE IN 1815

After the Congress of Vienna

Boundary of the German Confederation

ATLANTIC OCEAN

NORTH SEA

BALTIC SEA

BLACK SEA

AEGEAN SEA

ADRIATIC SEA

MEDITERRANEAN SEA

ENGLISH CHANNEL

KINGDOM OF GREAT BRITAIN

KINGDOM OF NORWAY AND SWEDEN

KINGDOM OF DENMARK

RUSSIAN EMPIRE

KINGDOM OF POLAND

PRUSSIA

MECKLEN-BURG

HANOVER

KINGDOM OF THE NETHERLANDS

OF

SAXONY

BADEN

WURTEM-BERG

BAVARIA

AUSTRIAN EMPIRE

SWITZERLAND

KINGDOM OF FRANCE

LOMBARDY

VENETIA

KINGDOM OF SARDINIA

TUSCANY

PAPAL STATES

MONTENEGRO

OTTOMAN EMPIRE

KINGDOM OF THE TWO SICILIES

KINGDOM OF SPAIN

KINGDOM OF PORTUGAL

empire, with long-range implications. While the countries of Europe were focusing their attention on the French Revolution and Napoleon, governors-general greatly extended British holdings in India. Among Britain's other important gains were the Cape of Good Hope and Ceylon from the Dutch; Malta; Mauritius in the Indian Ocean; and British Guiana and such islands as Trinidad, Martinique and Tobago in the New World. Although there was general agreement that problems not settled by the First Treaty of Paris in 1814 should be settled at the Congress of Vienna, England made it clear that the question of colonial possessions was not to be a topic for consideration. In earlier treaties of the period Britain had renounced colonial conquests it had made, but in 1815 it was in no mood to give a repeat performance.

Britain was able to extend its holdings in this way because, after the Battle of Trafalgar, it held undisputed mastery of the sea. Through this control it could for a century maintain a Pax Britannica. Until Germany threatened that control in the 20th century, no other world war broke out after the Napoleonic conflict. The political and economic face of the world, though vastly changed because of the Napoleonic period, was far removed from what Napoleon had pictured to himself.

In addition to the English gains, one of the most important overseas developments was the Latin-American movement for independence. Some of the states had achieved their independence by the time Napoleon fell; all of them felt the vitality of the movement, and all of them had obtained independence by 1825. The pretext for the actions of Spanish-Americans was that they owed allegiance only to the Bourbons, not to the Bonapartes. But when a Bourbon came back into power, the colonists decided that they did not owe allegiance to Ferdinand VII, either. The Brazilians did not reject the Portuguese ruling family, the Braganzas, so rudely, but in 1822 they declared their independence of Portugal while retaining one member of the family as emperor.

The Napoleonic period and regime made a most significant contribution to the United States, whose area was doubled by the acquisition of the Louisiana territory. Napoleon expected Latin America to look to the enlarged United States rather than to England.

Another result for the United States was the War of 1812, frequently called the second American war of independence, this time for economic independence of Great Britain. This war was a direct outgrowth of Napoleon's economic warfare with Great Britain, and in the long run redounded greatly to the advantage of the United States.

An attempt at a system of international organization was another important but unforeseen result of the Napoleonic period. All powers were agreed that Napoleon's endeavor to establish a universal monarchy must not be allowed to repeat itself. At Vienna they gave at least lip service to the idea of a balance of power. But of greater significance as a presage of the future was the Concert of Europe. (A Concert of Europe is an attempt to settle international problems by a series of congresses. Diplomats confer, much as Cabinet members meet regularly to discuss the problems of one country.) The Concert evolved out of the Quadruple Alliance, which was signed on the same day as the Second Treaty of Paris, November 20, 1815. The dimensions of the Napoleonic wars led the four victorious big powers to arrogate to themselves the right to settle the affairs of Europe. (The whole concept of "Great Powers," seen today in permanent membership in the Security Council of the United Nations, was an outgrowth of the Napoleonic wars.) The Concert failed because of its exclusive stress on trying to maintain the status quo, but still it was a decided break with the past.

The preponderance of power which Napoleon and France had possessed evoked, solely as a reaction, a previously nonexistent solidarity of ruling classes. This solidarity is shown particularly well in the Six Acts and the Carlsbad Decrees; the first suppressed any antigovernment manifestations in Britain, the latter attempted to choke off any breath of liberalism in the German Confederation.

Reference has already been made to the fact that Napoleon in his outlook, whether political or cultural, was a classicist. Yet his actions, plus his vicissitudes—the dramatic Hundred Days, the wintry retreat in 1812, the loss of his son to the custody of Austria—all made him the perfect subject for the Romantic poets. The Romantic attitude toward Napoleon is vividly revealed in a perhaps apocryphal conversation (later published in the spurious memoirs of Fouché) at the end of the spring campaign of 1813. When Napoleon asked Narbonne, his ambassador to Austria, "Well, what do they say of [the battle of] Lützen?" he received the reply, "Ah! Sire, some say you are a god, others, that you are a devil, but everyone allows you are more than a man."

Napoleon's policies did much to further Romantic ideas. One of these ideas was that the individual, within his own sphere, may do anything he pleases, without reference to convention; Napoleon himself certainly indulged in complete freedom of action. Romanticism also flourishes on nationalism; we have seen that Napoleon fostered nationalism both directly and indirectly, and that the whole nature of nationalism changed in the quarter century following the outbreak of the French Revolution.

Also romantic was the Napoleonic legend. Any legend must have a basis in fact, but it soon moves beyond the purely factual to distortion. Thus, because Napoleon was responsible for the Concordat, many later Frenchmen thought, erroneously, that he had given France religious freedom. To the fact that he gave France a glory unknown before or since was added the belief that his every war was a defensive one. In this jealously maintained legend the French people consider Napoleon in the way he wanted to be considered, as the consolidator of the French Revolution. The legend portrays him as the champion of liberty and of European federation; the upholder of universal manhood suffrage and a constitutional form of government; the maintainer of the peasant land settlement. In the mid-19th century liberals looked on Napoleon as the person who had rescued the Revolution from chaos. In addition, the legend affirms, correctly, that through his administrative system he bestowed on France an unprecedented unity.

The reflected prestige of the legend was the main reason that his nephew could become president of France in 1848. Napoleon III unquestionably did his best to model his regime on that of his uncle. The government established by his *coup d'état* of December 2, 1851, was almost exactly the same as that provided by the Constitution of the Year VIII. When he restored the Empire in 1852, he said, "Our actual society is no other thing but France regenerated by the Revolution of 1789 and organized by the emperor."

Each generation needs its heroes. Although the glamor of Napoleon may not have been an integral part of the Napoleonic revolution, it undoubtedly added to his impact on his own time and later years. Even stolid Queen Victoria ordered her son, the later Edward VII, to "kneel down before the tomb of the great Napoleon."

Napoleon has not been constantly a hero, but he has charmed individuals from generation to generation. Marshal Foch, no blind hero worshipper, said that he learned to read out of Thiers, whose *History of the Consulate and Empire* is very favorable to Napoleon. Fletcher Pratt, in the Preface of *The Empire and the Glory*, tells of seeing a movie in Paris in the mid-thirties, when French public opinion was pacifistic. The film did not deal with Napoleon, but his silhouette was shown once against a background of rolling smoke. The audience, several of whom stood at the sight, burst into wild applause. A correspondent for *Newsweek* witnessed a similar demonstration late in 1963. The French admire the grandeur of the Empire, as they admire the grandeur of De Gaulle in the Fifth Republic; and the Empire further had a humanness and warmth that the present regime lacks. The legend of Napoleon is still strong in France today.

It is no disparagement of Napoleon to say that he had lasting success only in those ventures which were in accord with historical development; this is true of the greatest of men. We must constantly keep in mind that other forces were at work at the same time. Economic forces, for example, continued to function and to promote industrial capitalism at the expense of Napoleonic mercantilism. Intellectual developments went on their way. But Napoleon was a motive force in the making of history. Although a creature of circumstance to the extent that a career such as his was possible only in a time of turmoil, Napoleon was far from being a mere creature of historical determinism. Goethe said he was one of the most productive men who ever lived; in Chateaubriand's estimation Napoleon was "the mightiest breath of life which ever animated human clay." Talleyrand, who was frequently at odds with his sometime chief, said, "In my opinion [he was] the most extraordinary man that has lived for many centuries." Napoleon aptly lived up to his own dictum: "It were better not to have lived at all than to leave no trace of one's existence behind."

Albert Guérard states, "No figure in history is more sharply defined than that of Napoleon I. But even in his case, man, career, and legend refuse to coincide." Pieter Geyl in his *Napoleon, For and Against*, declares: "History can reach no unchallengeable conclusions on so many-sided a character." Yet on one thing historians agree: the Napoleonic hallmark was enduringly stamped on France, on Europe, and beyond. Those who would have turned their faces to the past were forced, irresistibly, into a new era.

GUIDE TO FURTHER READING

The following essay will be restricted, except in a few cases where a French work in a particular area is superior to anything in English, to English-language works. The reason for this limitation is, first, a hope that the synthesis of this volume will encourage the reader both to delve more deeply and to spread more widely, and, second, a recognition that he will in all likelihood turn first to writings in his native tongue. (The deeper delving might take the form of reading periodical articles, none of which are cited here.) Although most of the writing on Napoleon has been done in French, there are enough works in English to satisfy even the most voracious reader.

For background, there is no better place to begin than with the three relevant volumes in "The Rise of Modern Europe" series. Leo Gershoy's *From Despotism to Revolution* (New York, 1944) treats the period from 1763 to 1789, not nearly so remote from Napoleon as one might think; Crane Brinton covers *A Decade of Revolution, 1789–1799* (New York, 1934) in interesting style; Geoffrey Bruun's *Europe and the French Imperium, 1799–1814* (New York, 1938), a balanced and judicious account, deals directly with the Napoleonic period. Louis Madelin, *The Consulate and the Empire* (2 vols.; New York, 1934–36) is interesting, fairly sound, and slightly pro-Napoleon. Volume IX in *The New Cambridge Modern History* (Cambridge, 1965), covering the period from 1793 to 1830, has various applicable sections and chapters written by specialists.

Recent biographies of Napoleon tend to be critical of him. Among these are J. C. Herold, *The Age of Napoleon* (New York, 1963) and J. M. Thompson, *Napoleon Bonaparte* (New York, 1952). The latter has both the virtues and defects of relying largely on Napoleon's correspondence, and also shows a strong pro-English bias. The shorter work of Felix Markham, *Napoleon and the Awakening of Europe*

THE NAPOLEONIC REVOLUTION

(London, 1954), offers some good insights and, despite its title, is an account of Napoleon's career. The same author has recently published in paperback a biography, *Napoleon* (New York, 1966), which incorporates the same good points as his other volume. Albert Guérard in *Napoleon I: A Great Life in Brief* (New York, 1956) limits himself strictly to biography and attempts to show the human side of Napoleon. Older but still extremely useful are the *Napoleon* of H. A. L. Fisher (New York, 1913) and that of Herbert Butterfield (London, 1939). Translation of *Napoléon* (4th ed.; Paris, 1953) by the late Georges Lefebvre, by all odds the best one-volume biography, is now under way.

The most recent detailed treatment of the military aspect of Napoleon's career is David Chandler's *The Campaigns of Napoleon* (New York, 1966), which includes relevant diplomatic developments and a section on Napoleon's theory of warfare. The maps in Vincent J. Esposito and John Robert Elting, *A Military History and Atlas of the Napoleonic Wars* (New York, 1964), are unsurpassed; the text shows more pro-Napoleon bias than good writing style. Both of these works are by teachers in military academies, but Chandler's will have more interest for the nontechnical student. *The Background of Napoleonic Warfare* (New York, 1957) by Robert Quimby is well worth its rather laborious reading. Works dealing in part with Napoleon's generalship include the eulogistic *Masters of Mobile Warfare* (Princeton, 1943) by Elbridge Colby, which goes only through Friedland, and Theodore Ropp's *War in the Modern World* (Durham, N.C., 1959). Although they do not deal exclusively with military matters, the volumes of Fletcher Pratt, *The Road to Empire: The Life and Times of Bonaparte, the General, 1795–1799* (New York, 1939) and *The Empire and the Glory: Napoleon Bonaparte, 1800–1806* (New York, 1949) are at their best in accounts of battles. Not sound history, they merit reading because of their fascination and splendid writing style. Another useful survey of Napoleon's military accomplishments is T. M. Hunter's *Napoleon in Victory and Defeat* (Ottawa, 1964). Liddell Hart's *The Ghost of Napoleon* (New Haven, Conn., 1934) stresses the view that Napoleon's main military impact resulted from later distortion of his ideas. J. F. C. Fuller's *The Conduct of War, 1789–1961* (New Brunswick, N.J., 1961) has three relevant and useful chapters, including one on Clausewitz, but is poorly written. The military maxims of Napoleon, published as *Napoleon and Modern War* (Harrisburg, Pa., 1949), must not be overlooked. François

Crouzet, *L'Économie britannique et le blocus continental* (*1806–1813*) (2 vols.; Paris, 1958) is by far the most thorough study made of Napoleon's economic warfare and revises the conclusions of such earlier works as Eli F. Heckscher, *The Continental System* (Oxford, 1922). Shepherd P. Clough has a chapter concentrating on the Continental System in *France: A History of National Economics, 1789–1939* (New York, 1939). William O. Shanahan's *Prussian Military Reforms, 1786–1813* (New York, 1954) shows the debt owed to Napoleon.

In the approximately two hundred pages devoted to the Napoleonic period in Jacques Godechot's *Les institutions de la France sous la Révolution et l'Empire* (Paris, 1951) the reader will find more worthwhile material than in any similar pagination. Although it overstates the case, *The Code Napoleon and the Common Law World* (New York, 1956), ed. by Bernard Schwartz, contains much useful material on the role and place of the Code. H. H. Walsh's *The Concordat of 1801* (New York, 1933), which stresses nationalistic considerations, remains the best single volume in English treating of Napoleon's relations with the Catholic Church. *The Emperor and the Pope,* by E. E. Y. Hales (Garden City, N.Y., 1961), confines itself almost exclusively to the personal relations, at the expense of historically important items. The best volume on Napoleon's educational system is F. V. A. Aulard, *Napoléon et le monopole universitaire* (Paris, 1911), a balanced and comprehensive account. Particularly valuable in Rondo E. Cameron's *France and the Economic Development of Europe, 1800–1914* (Princeton, N.J., 1961) is the chapter on "The Institutional Framework." R. B. Holtman, *Napoleonic Propaganda* (Baton Rouge, La., 1950), deals with thought control in France and its satellite areas.

Two books dealing with the satellite states have recently appeared. Gabriel H. Lovett, *Napoleon and the Birth of Modern Spain* (2 vols.; New York, 1964) is narrative and adds no new interpretations; the second volume is the more useful. Owen Connelly's *Napoleon's Satellite Kingdoms* (New York, 1965) is a well-rounded synthesis which fills what had been a gaping hole. To these should be added the old but very useful work of H. A. L. Fisher, *Studies in Napoleonic Statesmanship: Germany* (Oxford, 1903), which treats of the influence of the Napoleonic system on the German states.

A few volumes on the general nature of nationalism give perspective on the Napoleonic period. The introduction of Hans Kohn's *The*

THE NAPOLEONIC REVOLUTION

Idea of Nationalism (New York, 1944) is particularly good on the nature of nationalism. Boyd C. Shafer, *Nationalism: Myth and Reality* (New York, 1955) is of greatest value for the section "The Nation Becomes the People." Louis L. Synder, who uses an interdisciplinary approach in *The Meaning of Nationalism* (New Brunswick, N.J., 1954) should be noted especially for his treatment of the sentiment and classifications of nationalism. Eugene N. Anderson examines *Nationalism and the Cultural Crisis in Prussia, 1806–1815* (New York, 1939) through seven Prussian figures. Walter M. Simon shows how the Prussian reformers fell short of their goal and how some of their reforms were vitiated after 1815 in *The Failure of the Prussian Reform Movement, 1807–1819* (Ithaca, N.Y., 1955). Emiliana P. Noether puts the awakening of Italian national awareness during the Napoleonic period into proper perspective in *Seeds of Italian Nationalism, 1700–1815* (New York, 1951). William E. Robertson, *France and Latin-American Independence* (Baltimore, 1939) has two good chapters on nationalism in Central and South America during the time of Napoleon.

The most comprehensive volume on *The Diplomacy of Napoleon* is that of R. B. Mowat (New York, 1924). Harold C. Deutsch, *The Genesis of Napoleonic Imperialism, 1801–1805* (Cambridge, Mass., 1938) remains a standard work. Herbert Butterfield, *The Peace Tactics of Napoleon, 1806–1808* (Cambridge, England, 1929) continues the story chronologically. Paul F. Shupp, *The European Powers and the Near Eastern Question, 1806–1807* (New York, 1931) is carefully researched, but is lacking in interpretations and important conclusions. Far more valuable for Napoleon's activities in the Near East is Vernon J. Puryear, *Napoleon and the Dardanelles* (Berkeley, Calif., 1951).

Several volumes deal with the final diplomatic results of the Napoleonic period and the reaction to it. C. K. Webster, *The Congress of Vienna* (London, 1919) is a solid work; that of Harold Nicolson, *The Congress of Vienna* (New York, 1946), is based in part on Webster and is far more lively. G. Ferrero, *The Reconstruction of Europe: Talleyrand and the Congress of Vienna, 1814–1815* (New York, 1941), stresses the return to the balance of power. E. V. Gulick emphasizes the tie-up of theory and practice in *Europe's Classical Balance of Power* (Ithaca, N.Y., 1955). H. Kissinger, adding the idea of legitimacy to that of the balance of power, stresses the desire for stability in *A World Restored: Metternich, Castlereagh, and the Prob-*

lems of Peace, 1812–22 (Boston, 1957). For a study of the attempt at post-Napoleonic international organization, *The Aftermath of the Napoleonic Wars: The Concert of Europe—an Experiment* (New York, 1947) by H. G. Schenk is useful. One might also read in the fourth relevant volume of "The Rise of Modern Europe" series, Frederick B. Artz's *Reaction and Revolution, 1814–1832* (New York, 1934).

The impact of Napoleon would not have been complete without the Napoleonic legend. Albert Guérard deals with it, critically, in *Reflections on the Napoleonic Legend* (London, 1924). A major contribution to the legend was made by Napoleon's *Memoirs,* newly edited (New York, 1949) by Somerset de Chair. An accurate, non-legendary portrayal of Napoleon in the last five months of his life may be found in *Napoleon at St. Helena* (Garden City, N.Y., 1962), taken from the notebooks of General Henri G. Bertrand. After one has read enough to feel well-grounded in Napoleonic facts, Pieter Geyl's *Napoleon, For and Against* (New Haven, Conn., 1949) makes delightful and provocative reading. Geyl himself belongs in the anti-Napoleon school, as his comments on French historians of Napoleon make clear.

	Year II* 1793-94	Year III 1794-95	Year IV 1795-96
1 Vendémiaire	22 Sept. 1793	22 Sept. 1794	23 Sept. 1795
1 Brumaire	22 Oct.	22 Oct.	23 Oct.
1 Frimaire	21 Nov.	21 Nov.	22 Nov.
1 Nivôse	21 Dec.	21 Dec.	22 Dec.
1 Pluviôse	20 Jan. 1794	20 Jan. 1795	21 Jan. 1796
1 Ventôse	19 Feb.	19 Feb.	20 Feb.
1 Germinal	21 March	21 March	21 March
1 Floréal	20 April	20 April	20 April
1 Prairial	20 May	20 May	20 May
1 Messidor	19 June	19 June	19 June
1 Thermidor	19 July	19 July	19 July
1 Fructidor	18 Aug.	18 Aug.	18 Aug.
Sans-Culottides	17-21 Sept.	17-22 Sept.	17-21 Sept.

	Year V 1796-97	Year VI 1797-98	Year VII 1798-99
1 Vendémiaire	22 Sept. 1796	22 Sept. 1797	22 Sept. 1798
1 Brumaire	22 Oct.	22 Oct.	22 Oct.
1 Frimaire	21 Nov.	21 Nov.	21 Nov.
1 Nivôse	21 Dec.	21 Dec.	21 Dec.
1 Pluviôse	20 Jan. 1797	20 Jan. 1798	20 Jan. 1799
1 Ventôse	19 Feb.	19 Feb.	19 Feb.
1 Germinal	21 March	21 March	21 March
1 Floréal	20 April	20 April	20 April
1 Prairial	20 May	20 May	20 May
1 Messidor	19 June	19 June	19 June
1 Thermidor	19 July	19 July	19 July
1 Fructidor	18 Aug.	18 Aug.	18 Aug.
Sans-Culottides	17-21 Sept.	17-21 Sept.	17-22 Sept.

*The Republican calendar went into effect only with Year II; documents of the preceding year were redated from Gregorian to Republican. The first day of the Republican calendar coincided with the fall equinox.

Year VIII 1799-1800	Year IX 1800-01	Year X 1801-02	
23 Sept. 1799	23 Sept. 1800	23 Sept. 1801	1 Vendémiaire
23 Oct.	23 Oct.	23 Oct.	1 Brumaire
22 Nov.	22 Nov.	22 Nov.	1 Frimaire
22 Dec.	22 Dec.	22 Dec.	1 Nivôse
21 Jan. 1800	21 Jan. 1801	21 Jan. 1802	1 Pluviôse
20 Feb.	20 Feb.	20 Feb.	1 Ventôse
22 March	22 March	22 March	1 Germinal
21 April	21 April	21 April	1 Floréal
21 May	21 May	21 May	1 Prairial
20 June	20 June	20 June	1 Messidor
20 July	20 July	20 July	1 Thermidor
19 Aug.	19 Aug.	19 Aug.	1 Fructidor
18-22 Sept.	18-22 Sept.	18-22 Sept.	Sans-Culottides

Year XI 1802-03	Year XII 1803-04	Year XIII 1804-05	
23 Sept. 1802	24 Sept. 1803	23 Sept. 1804	1 Vendémiaire
23 Oct.	24 Oct.	23 Oct.	1 Brumaire
22 Nov.	23 Nov.	22 Nov.	1 Frimaire
22 Dec.	23 Dec.	22 Dec.	1 Nivôse
21 Jan. 1803	22 Jan. 1804	21 Jan. 1805	1 Pluviôse
20 Feb.	21 Feb.	20 Feb.	1 Ventôse
22 March	22 March	22 March	1 Germinal
21 April	21 April	21 April	1 Floréal
21 May	21 May	21 May	1 Prairial
20 June	20 June	20 June	1 Messidor
20 July	20 July	20 July	1 Thermidor
19 Aug.	19 Aug.	19 Aug.	1 Fructidor
18-22 Sept.	18-22 Sept.	18-22 Sept.	Sans-Culottides

Year XIV—1805

1 Vendémiaire	23 Sept. 1805	1 Frimaire	22 Nov. 1805
1 Brumaire	23 Oct. 1805	1 Nivôse	22 Dec. 1805

INDEX

INDEX

INDEX

INDEX

INDEX